THE CRYSTAL CHILDREN

THE CRYSTAL CHILDREN

*A Guide to the Newest Generation of
Psychic and Sensitive Children*

Doreen Virtue, Ph.D.

HAY HOUSE
Australia • Canada • Hong Kong • India
South Africa • United Kingdom • United States

First published and distributed in the United Kingdom by:
Hay House UK Ltd, 292B Kensal Rd, London W10 5BE. Tel.: (44) 20 8962
1230; Fax: (44) 20 8962 1239. www.hayhouse.co.uk

Published and distributed in the United States of America by:
Hay House, Inc., PO Box 5100, Carlsbad, CA 92018-5100. Tel.: (1) 760 431
7695 or (800) 654 5126; Fax: (1) 760 431 6948 or (800) 650 5115.
www.hayhouse.com

Published and distributed in Australia by:
Hay House Australia Ltd, 18/36 Ralph St, Alexandria NSW 2015. Tel.: (61) 2
9669 4299; Fax: (61) 2 9669 4144. www.hayhouse.com.au

Published and distributed in the Republic of South Africa by:
Hay House SA (Pty), Ltd, PO Box 990, Witkoppen 2068. Tel./Fax: (27) 11 467
8904. www.hayhouse.co.za

Published and distributed in India by:
Hay House Publishers India, Muskaan Complex, Plot No.3, B-2, Vasant Kunj,
New Delhi – 110 070. Tel.: (91) 11 4176 1620; Fax: (91) 11 4176 1630.
www.hayhouse.co.in

Distributed in Canada by:
Raincoast, 9050 Shaughnessy St, Vancouver, BC V6P 6E5. Tel.: (1) 604 323
7100; Fax: (1) 604 323 2600

© Doreen Virtue, 2003. Reprinted 2010.

Editorial supervisor: Jill Kramer   *Design:* Tricia Proctor

The moral rights of the author have been asserted.

The author of this book does not dispense medical advice or prescribe the use of
any technique as a form of treatment for physical or medical problems without the
advice of a physician, either directly or indirectly. The intent of the author is only
to offer information of a general nature to help you in your quest for emotional
and spiritual wellbeing. In the event you use any of the information in this book
for yourself, which is your constitutional right, the author and the publisher assume
no responsibility for your actions.

A catalogue record for this book is available from the British Library.

ISBN 978-1-8485-0197-3

Printed and bound in Great Britain by TJ International, Padstow, Cornwall.

CONTENTS

To the Crystal Children,
their parents, grandparents, and teachers.
Thank you for being angels
upon the earth, to help us all!

INTRODUCTION

Who Are the Crystal Children?

T he first thing you notice about Crystal Children (whom I'll also refer to as "Crystals") is their eyes—large, penetrating, and wise beyond their years. Their eyes lock upon yours hypnotically, while your soul is laid bare for these children to truly see.

Perhaps you've met this special new "breed" of kids who are rapidly populating our planet. They're happy, delightful, and forgiving. These new lightworkers, roughly newborn through age seven, are unlike previous generations. Ideal in many ways, they point to where humanity is headed . . . and it's a positive direction!

The older kids (approximately age 7 through 25), called "Indigo Children," share some characteristics with the Crystals. Both generations are highly sensitive and psychic, and they have important life purposes. The main difference is their temperament. Indigos have a warrior spirit, since their collective purpose is to mash down old approaches that no longer serve us. They're here to quash governmental, educational, and legal systems that lack integrity. To accomplish this end, they need hot tempers and fiery determination.

Adults who resist change and who value conformity may misunderstand the Indigos. They're often mislabeled with the psychiatric diagnoses of Attention Deficit with Hyperactivity Disorder (ADHD) or Attention Deficit Disorder (ADD). Sadly, when they're medicated, the Indigos often lose their beautiful sensitivity, spiritual gifts, and warrior energy. I wrote about the Indigos at length in my book *The Care and Feeding of Indigo Children;* and the subject was thoroughly explored in *The Indigo Children*, written by Lee Carroll and Jan Tober (both published by Hay House).

In contrast, the Crystal Children are blissful and even-tempered. Sure, they may have tantrums occasionally, but these kids are largely forgiving and easygoing. The Crystals are the generation who benefit from the Indigos' trailblazing. First, the Indigo Children lead with a machete, chopping down anything that lacks integrity. Then the Crystal Children follow the cleared path into a safer and more secure world.

The terms *Indigo* and *Crystal* were given to these two generations because they most accurately describe their aura colors and energy patterns. Indigo Children have a lot of indigo blue in their auras. This is the color of the "third-eye chakra," which is an energy center inside the head located between the two eyebrows. This chakra regulates clairvoyance, or the ability to see energy, visions, and spirits. Many of the Indigo Children have this gift.

The Crystal Children have beautiful, multi-colored, opalescent auras, in pastel hues like a quartz crystal's prism effect. This generation also harbors a fascination for crystals and rocks, as you'll read about later in this book. Hence, the name "Crystal Children."

The characteristics of Crystal Children are as follows:

- Are usually born in 1995 or later
- Possess large eyes with an intense stare
- Have magnetic personalities

- Are highly affectionate
- Start talking late in childhood
- Are very musically oriented, and may sing before talking
- Use telepathy and self-invented sign language to communicate
- May be diagnosed with autism or Asperger's syndrome
- Are even-tempered, sweet, and loving
- Are forgiving of others
- Are highly sensitive and empathetic
- Are very much connected to nature and animals
- Exhibit healing abilities
- Are quite interested in crystals and rocks
- Often discuss angels, spirit guides, and past-life memories
- Are extremely artistic and creative
- Prefer vegetarian meals and juices to "regular food"
- May be fearless explorers and climbers, with an amazing sense of balance

Children of the Millennium Shift

The year was 1995, a time when many of

us felt a gnawing restlessness in our bellies. On the heels of the materialistic '80s, we were searching for meaning, and avenues to contribute to the world's well-being. It was the beginning of a new spiritual renaissance, as we learned to look inward for answers and fulfillment.

Many individuals had profound spiritual experiences that year. I should know: It was on July 15, 1995, that an angel's loud, booming voice helped me escape unscathed from an attempted armed carjacking. Since that experience, I've devoted my life to teaching others about spirituality. And I've met countless people worldwide who also had major wake-up calls that year.

No wonder, then, that the Crystal Children started to arrive at that time. They knew that adults were finally ready for children's higher vibrations, and their purer way of living. Some older Crystal Children already existed on the planet. They were the scouts—the first generation of Crystals who came to check out the situation and report home during dreamtime transmissions. The earliest Crystals were the ones who signaled that 1995 was the year when the coast was clear for a large infusion of high-level babies. The number of Crystals born continues to escalate. And each year's crop of freshly born Crystal Children reveals increasingly profound spiritual abilities.

Misunderstood Gifts

As mentioned earlier, the generation preceding the Crystal Children are referred to as the Indigo Children, and they paved the way. One of the spiritual gifts of the Indigos is their ability to sniff out dishonesty, like a dog senses fear. Indigos *know* when they're being lied to, patronized, or manipulated. And since their collective purpose is to usher in a new world of integrity, the Indigos' inner lie detectors are integral. Again, this warrior spirit threatens some adults. Additionally, the Indigos are *unable* to conform to dysfunctional situations at home, work, or school. They don't have the ability to dissociate from their feelings and pretend that everything's okay . . . unless they're medicated or sedated.

Crystal Children's innate spiritual gifts are also misunderstood—specifically, their telepathic abilities, which often cause them to start talking long after most toddlers begin to do so.

In the new world that the Indigos are ushering in, we'll all be much more aware of our intuitive thoughts and feelings; we won't rely so much on the spoken or written word. Communication will be faster, more direct, and more honest, because it will be mind-to-mind. Already, increasing numbers of us are getting in touch with our psychic abilities. Our interest in the paranormal is at an all-time high, fueled by books, TV shows, and movies on the topic.

So it's not surprising that the generation following the Indigos are incredibly telepathic. As touched on above, many of the Crystal Children have delayed speech patterns, and it's not uncommon for them to wait until they're three or four years old to begin speaking. But parents have no trouble communicating with their silent children——far from it! Parents engage in mind-to-mind communication with their Crystal Children; and the Crystals use a combination of telepathy, self-fashioned sign language, and sounds (including song) to get their point across.

The trouble starts when the Crystals are judged by medical and educational professionals to have "abnormal" speaking patterns. It's no coincidence that as greater numbers of Crystals are being born, the number of diagnoses for autism is at a record high!

It's true that the Crystal Children are different from other generations, but why do we need to pathologize these differences? If the children are successfully communicating at home, and the parents aren't reporting any problems . . . then why create trouble where it doesn't exist?

The diagnostic criteria for autism is quite clear: The autistic person lives in his or her own world and is disconnected from other people. The autistic person doesn't talk because of an indifference to communicating with others.

Crystal Children are quite the opposite. As you'll read later on, they're among the most connected, communicative, caring, and cuddly of any generation. They're also quite philosophical and spiritually gifted—and they display an unprecedented level of kindness and sensitivity. For example, I received more stories than I could fit in this book about Crystal Children spontaneously hugging people in need. An autistic person wouldn't do that!

There are plenty of stories about great historical figures who started talking later in life—

Albert Einstein being among the most famous. Einstein's sister, Maja, noted that her brilliant brother didn't begin speaking until he was well over two years old. According to *U.S. News & World Report* (December 9, 2002), Einstein first uttered a sentence to complain that his milk was too hot. His stunned parents asked why he hadn't spoken earlier. "Because," the little genius supposedly replied, "previously everything was in order."

In my book *The Care and Feeding of Indigo Children,* I wrote that ADHD should stand for "Attention Dialed into a Higher Dimension." This would more accurately describe that generation of kids. In the same vein, Crystal Children don't warrant a label of autism. They aren't autistic—they're *awe*-tistic!

That's right—these children are worthy of awe, not labels of dysfunction. If anyone's dysfunctional, it's the systems that don't accommodate the continuing evolution of the human species. If we shame these children with labels or medicate them into submission, we'll have undermined a heaven-sent gift—we'll crush a civilization before it takes root. Fortunately, there are many positive solutions and alternatives.

And the same heaven that sent us the Crystal Children can assist those of us who are advocates for these kids.

The How and Why of This Book

I first became aware of the Crystal Children as I traveled around the world giving workshops about the angels. I noticed the Crystals' eyes and magnetic personalities. I held mental conversations with the children and could clearly hear them answering my questions telepathically. I'd watch them smile in response to my mentally projected compliments. *These kids hear my thoughts!* I realized.

Over the next few years, I interviewed children and parents for my book *The Care and Feeding of Indigo Children.* I've always been fascinated with finding patterns among human behavior. Although we're all as unique as snowflakes, the snowflakes share commonalities. With the Indigo Children, I noticed the traits described earlier. With the Crystal Children, my research took even more interesting twists and turns.

During this time, I received five or six unsolicited psychic readings from students and psychic associates who all told me the same thing: They saw that I was pregnant with a very special child. Well, I definitely *wasn't* pregnant; however, I now know that my psychic friends were seeing the Crystal Children around me. These Crystals were giving me messages that they wanted included in this book.

I found myself falling in love with each young Crystal Child I met. Their hearts were as open and loving as any angel with whom I'd interacted. I found them to be unguarded and unpretentious. I'd go to sleep thinking about the children, and wake up with volumes of information given to me by the spirit world (perhaps by the Crystals themselves?) while I slept.

Each morning I'd wake up knowing more about the Crystal Children than I'd previously known the evening before! I began lecturing about the Crystals and found my audiences very receptive. Many of them were parents, grandparents, or teachers of these special youngsters. They instantly recognized their children's characteristics as I described them.

I went on to ask audience members and subscribers of my newsletter to complete a questionnaire about their Crystals. Within one day of my putting out that request, I received hundreds of replies. For this book, I reviewed numerous stories submitted to me by people who are raising and teaching these remarkable children.

As I reviewed the survey results, two things happened. First, I felt my heart swell with love and gratitude. Just reading the stories made me feel as if I were in the presence of mighty angels! I felt a sense of ecstasy as I acknowledged these amazing kids' presence on our planet. I also felt reassured about our collective future. God wouldn't have sent this special breed of humans to Earth if we were on our last legs as a civilization or planet. Just as humans have evolved from ape-like postures, the Crystal Children provide concrete evidence that we're progressing from an evolutionary standpoint.

Second, I found clear—might I say *crystal* clear?—patterns among each survey respondent. I read dozens of similar stories about the Crystals and their relationships to animals, plants, rocks, and the elderly, for instance. I pored over many stories with eerily similar accounts about children telepathically communicating with their parents . . . while eschewing verbal communication.

Many parents told me, "I could never relate to the descriptions of Indigo Children. My youngster seemed different. But the Crystal Child profile—that one perfectly fit my child!"

Most parents reported a happy relationship with their Crystal Children marked by very few problems. I heard from parents and grandparents around the globe who described their Crystals as "angels," "the loves of my life," "true joys," and so on.

I noticed that not only were the Crystal Children highly spiritually sensitive, but so were their parents. The souls of Crystals were obviously selecting moms and dads who could raise them in a spiritually nurturing environment. Occasionally I met children who came through spiritually unaware parents. In these cases, their grandparents were highly evolved lightworkers who helped protect and hone the children's spiritual knowledge and gifts. Most parents told me that their Crystal Children were profound spiritual teachers who taught them a great deal about being exceptionally loving and kind.

One day I was lecturing about Crystals in Sydney, Australia. During the midday break, Reid Tracy, the president of Hay House (who was there selling my other books), asked me, "What's this book that everyone's asking me about? They all want to buy a Crystal Children book."

I laughed and told him that there was no such book yet; I was simply reporting the data I'd gathered from interviews and my own channelings. Reid remarked, "Well, they obviously want the book. Will you write it?" Without hesitation, I heard myself reply, "Yes, of course I will." You now hold the results of that decision in your hands!

Whether you're a parent, a parent-to-be, a grandparent, an educator, a health-care provider, or someone who's simply interested in children and spirituality, may this book provide validation and guidance for you and your Crystal Children!

— **Doreen Virtue, Ph.D.,**
Laguna Beach, California

· · · ✳ · · ·

CHAPTER ONE

In the Womb

It seems that everything involving Crystal Children is extraordinary, beginning with their conception. Several letter writers described how easily they conceived their Crystals. Mothers also told me that they communicated with their children prior to conception. Katharina, for instance, is a new mother of a nine-week-old boy. She says:

> "My son contacted me prior to his conception to let me know that he wanted to be born. He was conceived

in Glastonbury, England, one of the sacred places of this planet, which is often called Earth's heart chakra.

"I've heard that magic surrounds the Crystal Children, and this is certainly true for my son. Since his conception, many wonderful things have manifested for us on the physical plane, including a house in a very special place and an increased flow of money."

I also received several letters from grandmothers who had telepathic conversations with their unborn grandbabies.

Many of the women I surveyed and interviewed told me that their pregnancies were challenging, yet filled with magical spiritual experiences and personal growth. Several mothers described having telepathic communication with their unborn Crystal Children:

- One woman said that during her pregnancy, she received many messages from her unborn baby. The mother explained that while carrying her now four-month-old daughter, "she told us countless times that she was a girl, but we stubbornly didn't believe her. She also told us the exact date on which she would be born, and she was!"

- Another mother, Danica Spencer, said she had very potent dreams about powerful priestesses throughout her pregnancy (she later gave birth to a daughter).

- And Lori, the mother of 12-week-old Isabelle, had a physical healing during her pregnancy that she credits to her unborn child. Lori recalls:

> "I just knew from the moment of conception that my baby was very special and had so much love and light within her. Before becoming pregnant with Isabelle, I had some problems with abnormal cells found in my cervix, which were going to have to be removed after I gave birth.
> "While I was pregnant, they ran a Pap smear every couple of months to make sure that the cells weren't changing.

After the first test, all the abnormal cells were gone, and in every test thereafter, the cells couldn't be found, without any evidence that they'd ever been there! I know this happened because of the very special child growing inside of me.

"Often, Isabelle would come to me in my dreams and during my meditations. I could communicate with her long before she was born. There was also an amazing energy that you could feel radiating from my belly. The only way I can describe this energy is very bright, warm, glowing, and overflowing with love."

The Crystal Children have amazingly intense connections with nature, as you'll read about a little later. Cynthia Berkeley had a foreshadowing of her daughter's love for the water while she was pregnant with her. Cynthia says:

"I went swimming with the dolphins when I was pregnant with Leah, and ever since, she's had a natural affinity for water. While she was in the womb, Leah seemed to have conversations with the baby whales we saw on two separate days. She was just twisting and turning and kicking and vibrating in there!

"I've taken her swimming in the pool several times since she was an infant, and she always wants to put her head under the water. Leah loves it! At 15 months old, she's already trying to swim on her own."

Giving Birth

I received several letters from mothers who said that their Crystal Children telepathically communicated their correct date of birth. Kathy DiMeglio had a magical experience with Mother Mary that seemed to influence her daughter Jasmyn's birth date. Kathy said that during her pregnancy, she felt very connected to Mary, and learned that her birthday was September 8. Since this was eight days before Kathy's expected due date, she prayed to Mother Mary to help her give birth on September 8 instead.

Kathy says:

"I remember simply praying to Mary that our child be born on her birthday and letting it go at that. I forgot all about my prayer until I was in full hard labor at the hospital. At one point, I asked my husband what the date was, and he said, 'It's Thursday, September 8th.' I knew it was a miracle. I knew it was a gift. I even had a statue of Mary in the birthing room."

Several mothers said that they were struck by their newborn Crystal Child's eyes and magnetism from the moment of birth. For example, Andrea Kiger recalls:

"My three-year-old daughter, Abbie, has been different from the moment she was born. When I delivered her, they laid her on my chest and I was overcome with emotion, more so than with my first baby. As I sobbed, she calmly folded her hands and interlocked her fingers and just stared into my eyes. She didn't cry at all! The nurses were a little disturbed over this, as they all thought it was quite strange. I was almost frightened by the experience. I felt as though I were looking into the eyes of an ancient being. She never blinked, but just looked into me. I definitely felt that she was communicating with me."

The Crystal Children have an authoritative air about them, as if they're wise adults in little bodies. Even more, they seem like seasoned sages . . . little sorcerers and high-priestesses. The power that they exert from infancy can hold sway over adults. This power doesn't come from brute force, though, but from steely determination and crystal-clear intentions. When parents first encounter their children's power, it can take them aback.

Lisa Roulet is the mother of 20-month-old Kaitlyn, who exhibited remarkable personal power just days after she was born. Lisa explains:

"Kaitlyn was born three and a half weeks early. She slept almost all the time for the first three weeks. When she was just six days old (and should have still been in the womb), I first became aware of her extraordinary presence and power. On that day, against my better judgment, I listened to other people's advice to try to keep her awake more. When I nudged her, Kaitlyn gave me a strong look communicating power, confidence, and authority that told me in no uncertain terms to stop bothering her and let her sleep. I honestly felt that I was in the presence of a deity that night."

The Crystal Children do share characteristics such as charisma and magnetism with deities, which you'll read about in the next chapter. These traits are undoubtedly part of the package that will make them great leaders in the future.

· · · ✳ · · ·

CHAPTER TWO

Oh, Those Eyes!

As I touched on earlier, the most distinctive trait of the Crystal Children is their intense, wide-eyed stare. They seem to see *everything* with those big eyes! Sometimes their gaze is unnerving, as they seem to lay bare your soul's secrets. As they lock eyes with yours, it feels like a high-level being is scanning you.

Penny describes her two-year-old daughter, Samantha, as having "eyes that seem to go straight through to your soul."

Many mothers reported that their Crystal Child had intense eyes from day one.

Keli Carpenter says that from the moment of her son Dakota's birth six months ago, he's looked intensely into people's eyes "as if he's speaking to you. Everyone comments on it."

Dakota's grandmother, Wynona, adds, "He looks very deeply into my eyes, and it feels as if he can see into my very soul. Just a couple of days after he was born, he stared into my eyes for more than 20 minutes." Wynona said that she found herself speaking to him in her mind, and it felt as if he were communicating with her in some way—that he "knew the truth of me and all things. It felt strange and exciting at the same time."

Another Crystal Child's mother, Pam Caldwell, expressed similar sentiments:

> "Since the second that Hannah came out, she just stared at me with her dark and piercing eyes, searching my eyes and soul. It was very penetrating—not uncomfortable at all, but deep. She was so aware even from her first minute! She's made many people in the grocery store uncomfortable because of her intense gaze. It's not creepy. It's just so

obvious that Hannah can see right through people and read them."

These observations about the Crystal Children's eyes aren't just rooted in parental pride. Kelly Colby-Nunez has five children, and she notices a definite difference in the eyes of her three younger children (ages 6, 4, and 15 months). Kelly says about her younger children, "One look into their eyes and you know they're highly intelligent and have more wisdom than the older children and us adults. Their eyes just sparkle like light reflecting off crystal. People comment on this all the time."

Crystals' eyes reflect their deep spiritual understanding. They're loving, patient, and kind eyes—like those of angels. Nadia Leu is the mother of Celeste, age 18 months. Nadia recalls, "From the first look she gave us, Celeste seemed to be so wise and compassionate, so understanding, and at the same time so above all human suffering. From the time of her birth on, she's had a very strong and knowing look in her eyes, and her demeanor has always been very calm and assured in all situations."

These expressive and intense eyes are one reason why Crystal Children start talking later in life, as they communicate so much through their eyes alone. Their eyes are part of the mesmerizing power that Crystal Children have over grown-ups as well. Many parents told me that their children's eyes hypnotized adults. For instance, Phillipa said that her 18-month-old daughter, Isabella, creates quite a stir with her eyes. She says, "No matter where we go, people stop in their tracks to come close to Isabella, to be in her energy and to look into her crystal-blue eyes. In most instances, they become totally captivated. Once Isabella locks eyes with someone, it's very hard for them to look away—until my daughter is good and ready to let them go."

Magnetic Personalities

The Crystal Children's magnetism is reminiscent of those old-fashioned hypnotists who would say, "Look into my eyes . . . deeply, deeply, look into my eyes!" However, the Crystals' stares aren't manipulative. These children are merely gathering information about humans and the planet. They're also sending out messages of love through their eyes, and this energy is a gift that we desperately need right now.

The Crystal Children see past the surface of people. They see the inner Divine light, and their eyes are open in awe as they take everything in.

The love radiating from the Crystals is irresistible. Even people who normally shy away from kids are drawn to the warm personalities of the Crystal Children.

Lori, the mother of 12-week-old Isabelle, whom we met earlier, says the attention her daughter attracts is unusual—even for a cute baby! Lori explains:

> "People are very attracted to her. Now I know that people love babies and are very interested in them, but this is different. Isabelle seems to draw others to her like a magnet of pure love and light. Everyone always seems to have the same comments about her.

They always say how beautiful she is, and yes, all babies are beautiful . . . but not like this. There's something so special about her that just radiates from within, a truly loving glow about her that makes her especially beautiful. Isabelle also has the most incredible eyes. They're so filled with love, understanding, and wisdom."

The Crystal Children are giving healing doses of love to people wherever they go. They're like mobile energy healers, pushed in strollers by parents who may not realize the important function they're playing in taking their children out in public.

Stephanie and Mark Watkeys of New South Wales, Australia, are the proud parents of 13-month-old Bryn. The Watkeys say:

"Bryn magnetically attracts people wherever he goes. All sorts of people speak to him and just want to be around him. Our son is an absolutely delightful child, full of laughter and light, and he has the full attention of people wherever he goes. He's very sociable and animated. Everyone who meets him comments on how alert he is. It's as if his eyes are drinking in everything and everyone around him. At 13 months, he has the look of a wise old man, yet the lightheartedness of a happy baby!"

And Victoria's grandmother reports that her three-year-old granddaughter has always been aware of things, and that she's bright and sensitive far beyond her years. "Victoria is always the center of attention, even when she doesn't say a word," her grandmother says. "Perfect strangers are drawn to her and speak with her without any apparent provocation."

This phenomenon points to the origination and purpose of the Crystal Children. Their high-level spiritual frequencies and their ego-free personalities indicate that they're very spiritually evolved. Where did they come from? They share similarities with the accounts of extraterrestrials who have large eyes and small mouths and who communicate telepathically. Yet, the warmth of the Crystal Children exceeds the reports of the mechanical energy emitted in most extraterrestrial (E.T.) encounters.

Perhaps we're meeting a hybrid type of incarnated angel, masquerading as beautiful little boys and girls. Yet one thing's certain: These children are here to both teach us and to save us . . . from ourselves. But we must *help* the Crystal Children to help us. The first step is to understand their uniquely wonderful qualities.

CHAPTER THREE

Late-Talkers, Telepathy, and Trances

At age two, Harry was diagnosed as "autistic" when it was apparent that his speech development lagged behind normal. At first, his parents and doctor thought that Harry had a hearing problem, so they had grommets (protective loops) placed in his ears. But Harry still didn't speak. His mother, Karenanne, says:

> "Harry has always had a very sunny temperament and showed no angst at being unable to speak. It was like talking was something he'd do when he was good and ready. It was the

same with his reading skills. He showed no interest in baby books, yet when he got interested in Pokemon, he rapidly showed that he indeed knew how to read, and he just pored over those handbooks."

At age five, Harry began to speak. It was as if his reading and writing skills were awakened after lying dormant for many years. Now at age nine, Harry reads children's encyclopedias for fun and has developed a good general knowledge for his age.

Was Harry autistic previously? His personality doesn't indicate that. Remember that autism describes a condition where people live in their own little worlds, disconnected from others. They don't speak because they don't *notice* others.

Harry, in contrast, quite frequently asks strangers questions, and he'll approach other children to inquire about a toy they're carrying. Harry's mother says that she's gotten used to her son approaching strangers now. "And the surprising thing is," she remarks, "that people sense his loving energy and accept it without getting angry at the invasion of their space. He's showing them how to be more open."

So why was Harry diagnosed as autistic? Does speaking or reading later than expected warrant such a serious diagnosis? Why not call these sensitive children "late-talkers" instead of pathologizing them with psychiatric diagnoses and making them feel ashamed of themselves?

Hundreds of parents around the globe have submitted stories for this book, telling about their Crystal Children who "took their sweet time" to begin speaking. Perhaps instead of labeling this phenomenon "an epidemic of autism," as the media and medical establishment has done, we should examine it for indications of humankind's evolution.

Who knows—maybe we don't need speaking anymore! Perhaps it's as antiquated as the toes that we once used for climbing trees! Could telepathy be akin to the opposable thumbs we developed through evolution—that is, a necessary new tool for a changing world?

Truly, speech does seem clumsy and imprecise compared to mental communication. Many scientists at large universities such as Stanford, Princeton, and Yale have studied the phenomenon of mind-to-mind communication. These studies yield verifiable data supporting the premise that telepathy is a measurable behavior that definitely exists. I wrote about this scientific research in my book *The Lightworker's Way* (Hay House, 1997).

I remember my initial (big) experience with telepathy. I was 17, and my beloved grandfather had just been killed in an auto accident. An hour after his death, his apparition came to me. I was wide-awake, sober, and in full communication with him. He had a bluish-white glow around him but otherwise looked just like he always had. Then he began speaking to me—not with his mouth, but with his mind. I heard his voice inside my head as plainly as if he were alive and talking into my ear. He told me not to grieve for him, that he was fine. We communicated a bit more, and then he was gone. My grandfather's brother, who lived in a distant city, also reported seeing his spirit that same night.

That incident taught me to trust the mental communications that I'd regularly received throughout my life from angels and the spirit world. It helped me when I became a full-time psychic medium years later. And it continues to assist me in my writing and speaking work. When people compliment me on my psychic abilities or prolific writing abilities, I always reply, "Thank you. I'm a good listener."

Being a parent to a Crystal Child means being a good listener as well. In fact, just having a Crystal seems to awaken latent psychic abilities in parents. Andrea Kiger calls her three-year-old daughter, Abbie, "a classic Crystal Child" because she matches the description so perfectly. Andrea says that not only did she give birth to this special little being, but she also gave birth to her own psychic abilities. She recalls, "Out of nowhere I was able to know things, and see and communicate with those who have passed over. This all came about the very day after Abbie's birth. I'm certain that it was an awakening for me."

Those who have had near-death experiences report an increase in psychic abilities afterward. Many also say that being in the presence of great love, such as that which exists in the afterlife plane, opens us up psychically. So it's not surprising that parenting a super-loving Crystal Child would have this same effect.

Crystals also choose psychically sensitive parents and grandparents as part of their "survival on Earth" techniques. After all, if kids aren't going to communicate verbally, they need to choose telepathic moms and dads to ensure that their needs are met.

As I've mentioned, it's very common for Crystal Children to begin speaking at age three or later. This was the case for Teresa Zepeda, whose six-year-old daughter is fittingly named "Crystal." Teresa says:

> "Crystal only spoke three words (*Mama, Dada, no*) up until age three, when she suddenly started using complete sentences. Prior to that age, she used grunts and charades. We called her 'cave baby.' But she also had a way of letting us know what she wanted without saying anything. I guess she was communicating with telepathy. It had to be. How else would I know what she was thinking?"

Teresa's daughter exemplifies a pattern that many parents describe, whereby the children go from minimal verbalization to more comprehensive speaking skills virtually overnight. Catherine Poulton says that her son Kylan, age five, was about three years old before he could talk. "Kylan didn't speak, didn't even form nouns, and then suddenly one day he started talking in complete sentences."

The issue of late-talking only seems to be a problem for those who worry. For more relaxed parents, it's a non-issue. Such is the case for Beverly Moore, mother of Ethan, age five. Beverly says that "Ethan didn't talk until he was about age three. He never had the 'baby talk' sound either. I wasn't too concerned, as I figured he'd speak when he had something to say. I never had a problem knowing what Ethan wanted."

However, it's not always easy for parents to nonchalantly accept that their children are "different." One woman told me that she feels embarrassed around other mothers because she suspects that they judge her for having a "mute" son. So some parents take the matter into their own hands, doing research, reading all the books about late talking, and instituting behavioral and dietary modifications to spur their children's language development. Evie says that her two-year-old daughter, Mei, responded positively to homeschooling. She says:

"Mei was a happy and alert baby who walked at ten months, yet she decided not to speak until later, and we had to evaluate her for speech impairments. She tested very highly in the social and cognitive areas, but she just wouldn't speak. At around 15 months, she spoke a few words here and there. In fact, her first word was 'Hi!' The doctor said that she was about four months behind in speaking. So I worked with her at home, and now she talks a lot. At age two, she knows all of her colors, letters, and the numbers one through ten."

Several mothers told me that their Crystal Children appreciated the extra attention that homeschooling provided, and that the kids' vocabularies grew as a result.

Still, there are many ways to communicate. Many parents commented that their children created their own form of sign language. One woman said that her child went through deliberate motions to teach her this self-styled way of communicating so that they could understand each other. Kelly Colby-Nunez says that her youngest children prefer to communicate through drawings: "My children (ages 6, 4, and 15 months) prefer drawing to speaking and will spend hours doing so. My six-year-old also told me that he often communicates with his friends without talking."

Perhaps one reason why Crystal Children speak later than previous generations is that verbal speech is foreign to them. This is what Sue Jalil suspects about her four-year-old son, Sean:

> "Sean's very telepathic, and his speech was late in developing, so late that he had a grommet put in to help him hear better. It's only recently that he's managed to overcome some of the speech difficulty. Even now, though, some letters are very hard for him to form. I believe that this is his first time on planet Earth, and that to use his mouth and tongue to communicate is

very foreign to him, where in the past he was just telepathic. By the way, the grommet made no difference whatsoever."

Many parents and doctors suspect that late-talkers have a medically based hearing problem. Penny said that both of her daughters didn't talk until they were three years old. She had both girls' ears tested, which revealed that their hearing was fine. Penny says that she hadn't really been worried, though:

"Something told me that the problem wasn't with their hearing. My instincts told me that my children just didn't feel an overwhelming need to talk yet. My oldest seemed to have a language all her own. We didn't understand what she was saying, but she was talking all the time. And with both girls, I always seemed to know what they wanted or needed."

Penny says that her biggest challenge with her Crystals was how others perceived them. She recalls:

"People would ask my kids questions about things, and they wouldn't answer or didn't know. There are certain expectations when people talk to a child that age, but my children didn't fit those. For example, I would try to teach them how old they were or where their nose was, and they were totally uninterested in learning these things."

Penny remembers feeling embarrassed and judged when her children wouldn't answer people's questions. She recalls that the baby-sitter turned her in to Children's Protection Services because her daughters didn't talk much and were barking and pretending that they were dogs.

Like many Crystal Children, Penny says that her daughters' motor skill development was right on track, but their verbal skills lagged behind, in comparison to the norm. Yet, when each girl reached the age of three, they suddenly opened up and began speaking normally. Penny says, "I never had any doubt that they were bright kids. I have to keep reminding myself that it's okay that my children are different. They're going to be very special people. I just know it."

The parents who seem to have the easiest time with their late-talking children are those who learn to communicate telepathically, and who recognize and use body language. A mother who's actually named Crystal says, "My daughter's almost two. She doesn't speak yet and doesn't feel the need to. We can look at each other and know what the other wants, so for now it seems that speech isn't necessary."

Another mother named Misty Rose had an easy time communicating nonverbally with her daughter, Leah. However, Misty says, "When Leah was 12 months old, we had to remind her that not everyone could communicate with her telepathically, so she had to use her words."

That bit of information seemed to help. Now two, Leah speaks at the level of three- and four-year-olds. Part of the pact that parents have with Crystal Children is showing them "the ropes" of living on Earth.

Telepathic Communication

The Crystal Children are born psychic. As

babies, their heads and eyes turn as they clearly see angels and spirit guides. With inborn spiritual gifts, it's normal for them

Crystal Children are born psychic.

to be profound mind-readers as well. Many parents told me stories similar to Natarsha's.

Natarsha is the mother of five-year-old Tyrique. She says that her son's statements have always stunned her. Natarsha exclaims, "I swear he reads my mind!"

One day the two were riding on a bus in silence. Natarsha mentally wondered whether Tyrique would spend the upcoming weekend with his dad. Suddenly, Tyrique blurted out, "Dad's picking me up on Friday to go to his house."

The following day, Natarsha was thinking about what to make for dinner when Tyrique said, "Mom, I have a good idea. Why don't you make that rice dish for dinner?"

When Natarsha asked Tyrique how he knew what she was thinking, he replied, "God told me in my head."

Tyrique's spiritual listening skills have

proven handy on more than one occasion. Natarsha was dressing for work one day, struggling to zip up her pants. They weren't tight; they just weren't zipping. Just then, Tyrique entered the room and said, "Mommy, you have to button your pants first and then the zipper will work." Natarsha wondered how Tyrique even knew that she was having problems with her zipper.

She says, "I thought I'd humor him by complying with his statement, so I buttoned my pants as he watched me, and then tried the zipper, thinking, *This isn't going to work.*" The zipper went up without a hitch! When Natarsha asked Tyrique how he knew to come to the bathroom to help her, he simply stated, "I just know. I listen to my mind," and he walked off. To this day, Natarsha has to button those pants for the zipper to work.

§ § §

The Crystal Children teach us to trust our intuitive thoughts and feelings. Like Natarsha, Carolyn asked her six-year-old daughter, Haley, about her telepathic abilities. Haley replied that she could see into her mother's brain and also see her thoughts.

I've taught psychic-development classes worldwide since 1996, and I've found that one of the most important things to do when trying to develop psychically is to notice and trust the thoughts, feelings, words, and visions that enter your mind. The Crystal Children are brilliant role models for doing so. Jaimie says that her 18-month-old daughter, Isabella, confidently announces, "Daddy, Daddy" moments before her father arrives home. Often when the telephone rings, she says, "Nanny," and sure enough, her grandmother is on the phone.

One reason why children are so psychic is their indifference to whether they're merely imagining these intuitive messages. They don't anguish about whether something is make-believe or real. To children, it's *all* real!

The Crystal Children are clearly mind-readers. Magda says that her four-year-old daughter frequently verbalizes what she's thinking. "For instance," she recalls, "one evening I saw her sleeping in bed and thought, *I love you*, and she replied in her sleep, 'I love you, too!'"

As Crystals grow up, this telepathy can either be polished or squelched. The former happens when parents praise the child's gift and learn how to develop it in themselves. The latter occurs when parents show fear or anxiety in response to their child's ability to read minds.

Telepathy is part of the Crystal Children's Divine arsenal to help rid the earth of deceit. When someone is fully telepathic, no one can lie to them. As the Crystal Children progress into adulthood, they'll know with certainty if a politician or salesperson is deceiving them. Collectively, they'll compel the inhabitants of our planet to live with integrity.

Telepathy has a more immediate benefit as well. Crystal says that she uses telepathy to communicate with her three-year-old daughter, Zoey, in emergency situations. For instance, if Zoey strolls away from her, Crystal telepathically shouts "Stop!" and Zoey immediately halts and turns to look at her mother.

Going into Trances

Sometimes Crystal Children go into trances where they seemingly don't hear their parents. This can happen particularly when they're outside in nature. This trancelike state is a characteristic often used to diagnose autism.

But with Crystal Children, this would be an inaccurate diagnosis, because these kids are just tuning out the world *temporarily*. Not only that, but Crystal Children are very empathetic, connected, and loving with other people. Truly autistic kids exhibit no sense of connection at all with the outside world.

Personally, I go into trances when I'm channeling or receiving information. Before I fully acknowledged my spiritual gifts, I actually received many angel messages while watching television. That's because television focuses the mind on a single spot, in much the same way that scrying mirrors (black mirrors used for divination) and crystal balls are focal points.

Andrea says that her three-year-old daughter, Abbie, also goes into trances when she watches television. Andrea explains:

> "When the television set is on, Abbie gets 'sucked in' to the point where she can't hear anyone around her. We really have to limit her TV time. Abbie is a gentle soul and healer who's one with nature and animals. As much as technology goes

against who she is, she seems to get sucked into it and can't escape its grip. We have to turn off computers and TVs to get her to interact with the family again."

Another mother, Denise Bunning, said that her daughter Alice used to go into trances when she was younger. Denise would use her hands to turn Alice's face toward her to get her full attention. Now at age five, Alice uses the same method with her mother. Whenever Denise ignores her daughter, the little girl turns her mother's face toward her own!

As touched on above, many parents told me that their children become incredibly focused—as if they're in a trance—when they're outside in nature. The Crystal Children sit and stare at bugs or leaves for minutes at a time. This focusing ability is a gift that the Crystals will find useful in the future as they assume leadership roles as adults.

· · · ❋ · · ·

CHAPTER FOUR

A High Degree of Sensitivity

Crystal Children rely on their intuition to discern the truth about people and situations instead of making assessments based on physical appearance or judgments. Their intuition is like radar, constantly scanning their surroundings. Nobody can hide their true thoughts, feelings, or intentions from the Crystal Children's exquisite awareness. Nor can these kids hide from an awareness of the truth, even if they'd rather not know it. Sometimes sensitivity can seem more like a curse than a blessing. Sensitive people may inadvertently absorb negative energies, and they can be adversely affected by them.

Danica says that her son, Koa, is three years old and highly sensitive. Danica's greatest challenge is figuring out how to help her son when others' energy affects him. She says:

> "Koa is so sensitive that if anyone's angry, frustrated, or experiencing any strong emotions (even if no one else would notice or if they're concealing it), he'll act it all out. It's difficult parenting highly sensitive children because they're so affected by their surroundings.
>
> "Now that we have a wonderful home with excellent energy, our son is a dream. In some of the previous places we've lived, the energy of the house alone was often cause for crying and confusion. Koa does best when surrounded by positive energy, and it's crucial for him to be in a house with good energy flow."

One way to ensure that your home projects good energy is to practice the ancient Chinese art of room placement called Feng Shui. Space-clearing is another method. The former is described in wonderful detail in *The Western Guide to Feng Shui* by Terah Kathryn Collins, and I write about the latter in my book *Angel Therapy* (both are published by Hay House).

Sensitive to World Energies

The Crystal Children are very much affected by the collective energy of the planet. When masses of people become afraid, or if a world-changing event is afoot, Crystals may become depressed or agitated.

Sara says that her son, Zak, was two years old on September 11, 2001. They live in London, so the attacks occurred at about 10 P.M. their time. Zak had been asleep since 7:00 P.M. Sara heard the news about the Twin

> The Crystal
> Children
> are very much
> affected by the
> collective energy
> of the planet.

Towers on the news as it happened, and moments later, she heard strange noises coming from Zak's bedroom.

Sara ran to her son's room and recalls the terrifying moments that followed:

"He was in a terrible state, clawing at his neck and fighting for breath! I'd never seen anything like that before! I heard a disembodied voice say, 'Call an ambulance!' which I did. When the ambulance arrived, the emergency team took one look at Zak and said, 'Code blue!' and rushed him to the hospital. Inside the ambulance, Zak struggled to breathe, and I feared he was about to leave the planet."

Zak was turning blue by the time they arrived at the hospital, and the doctors said he was having a life-threatening croup attack. Sara recalls, "I knew it was terribly serious as I looked around at the doctors, who were ashen. I was guided to remove my crystal necklace and hold it over Zak, praying that he would heal.

And he did. The doctors later told me that it was the worst case of croup they'd ever seen."

An American Crystal Child named Chad was also highly empathetic to the global situation that was precipitated by September 11. A first-grader, Chad wrote about his feelings:

"My dream is to help the people of Afghanistan. They're dying. Even though they have killed many of the people in our country, you should treat other people the way you want to be treated. You should help your neighbors. They have many sicknesses. It is sad that a ton of people did that, but I forgive them."

Parents who worry that their children are depressed, hyper, or anxious should check to see if world events are affecting them. Many children are impacted unconsciously by the world's energy. Invoke Archangel Michael to watch over your kids, or ask Mother Mary (both are nondenominational) to comfort them. Talk to your children, and allow them to express their fears and frustrations openly.

The Nature of Sensitivity

The generations prior to the Indigos and Crystals had the ability to pretend that everything was great even if it wasn't. The new children—especially the Crystals—don't have the option of going into denial. They feel others' emotions as if they were their own.

Catherine says that her three-year-old daughter is one of the most observant people she's ever met. She points out, "Nothing slips by her. My daughter is very attuned to people and their emotions. In fact, my husband and I must be very careful if we disagree in front of her, because she tries to mediate for us and isn't content until everyone is at peace. She keeps asking, 'Are you happy?' until we truly are."

The Crystal Children are here as peace-keepers, and they tune in when someone isn't at peace. According to their mothers, Taylor, Emily, William, and Zoey are all three-year-olds who reflect this characteristic:

- Taylor stops whatever he's doing when another child cries. He'll ask, "What's wrong?" and inquire how he can help. Every day, he reports to his parents which children were crying at preschool, and why. It's as if his focus is on helping those who are sad.

- Emily doesn't have a huge vocabulary, but when she does speak, she tends to focus on emotions. Her mother, Wendy, says, "Emily is highly perceptive about the emotions boiling up in grownups, and somehow she possesses the language and the skills to label them and point them out (despite my efforts to shield my emotions and thoughts from her)."

- William gets his feelings hurt easily, and he's crushed when he thinks he's done something wrong but wasn't aware of it.

- Zoey hugs and consoles anyone she sees crying. She says to them, "It's okay, it's all right, want me to kiss you better?" And she tells everyone she meets that she loves them.

Rihana and Isabelle are acutely sensitive as well:

- Rihana, 12 months, cries terribly whenever she believes she's hurt someone else, emotionally or physically.

- Isabelle, 12 weeks old, gets upset very quickly if she's around angry or negative people, yet her mother adds: "Isabelle brings a peace and calm to people. Her energy is so strong and loving that she has an instant calming effect on them."

Sensitive Bodies

Not only are the Crystal Children emotionally sensitive, but they're also physically sensitive. They can easily become overwhelmed by too much stimuli.

- *Crystal Children are sensitive to loud noise.* Penny says that her two- and four-year-old daughters become very upset if someone raises their voice in anger. She says, "I'm more careful now about how I communicate with the girls if I'm upset. Knowing that they feel emotions so strongly, I have to be careful about the volume or the intensity of anger in my voice."

- *Crystal Children are sensitive to crowds.* Beth says that her three-year-old son, Taylor, can't handle being in large crowds. She recalls, "He's had this trait since birth. His preschool recently had a back-to-school night, and Taylor wanted nothing of it—too much activity and noise, so he just ran outside and stood under a tree eating a cookie."

- *Crystal Children are sensitive to temperature.* Cathy notices that her son, William, age three, feels cold more easily than other people.

- *Crystal Children are sensitive to clutter and disorganization.* When Haley, six, feels that her room is too messy, she cleans it and announces: "I need a space clearing!" Her mother then gives her a special bell to ring to clear the energy. After Haley ceremoniously rings the bell, she says, "Mom, now the energy in my room is awesome!"

- *Crystal Children are sensitive to chaotic environments.* Mei, age two, becomes hyper when she's in a place with heightened activity, like a shopping mall at Christmastime. Her mother says that at home she's never hyper.

- *Crystal Children are sensitive to artificial ingredients and chemicals.* Jaimie says that her 18-month-old daughter, Isabella, has very sensitive skin. Jaimie explains:

> "I only use natural ingredients on her skin now because it becomes dry when exposed to commercial soap. We use Evening Primrose Oil soap instead. She always reacts better to natural remedies, and luckily my local pharmacist creates herbal remedies for many childhood ills. Isabella always vomits when she takes over-the-counter medication. She can't keep it down; her little body always rejects it like a reflex. However, she tolerates herbal medicines just fine."

Seemingly Unbreakable

Fortunately, angels watch over the sensitive Crystal Children. Many of them seem to be unbreakable, impervious to harm.

Tori's mother says that even though her four-year-old daughter plays rough with their pets, she always emerges unscathed. For example, Tori will lie on the floor while the family's big dogs trample about her, but she's only gotten a couple of minor scratches. And her large male cat bites *at* her but never leaves a mark.

And Andrea reports that her six-month-old daughter, Abbie, once escaped harm against all odds. Andrea explains, "I was carrying Abbie when I slipped on some black ice in a parking lot." Andrea was horrified as her baby daughter lay facedown on the pavement, not moving at all. So Andrea quickly turned Abbie over, only to find that her daughter was smiling, without a scratch on her.

Andrea says that Abbie has had many close calls when it comes to accidents, but somehow has never been hurt. "It's almost like she's unbreakable physically, although emotionally she is *so* sensitive. She doesn't like loud noise, people fighting, violence, rough play, or red meat."

So, Crystal Children can afford to be sensitive . . . they're protected—their ever-so-important life purpose ensures that heaven watches over them. Those who do get injured may go through that experience as part of their contract for spiritual growth.

Many of the parents who wrote to me said that these children are not only impervious to injury, but they're also fearless. Perhaps one reason is that they expect the best. Their optimism attracts experiences of safety and protection.

No Fear

The little boy was amazing! As I sat outside at a resort hotel in Kona, Hawaii, I couldn't take my eyes off this one kid. Dressed in an outfit so colorful that it would have made Joseph's dreamcoat look dull by comparison, the boy was walking on walls—I mean, literally!

I figured that this kid was about seven years old, and he walked along the edges of the hotel's three-foot concrete wall like he was a four-wheel-drive truck. The wall's edge was narrower than the boy's foot, but no matter. The boy confidently walked without hesitation and didn't even come close to falling. Finally, his grandfather grew tired of watching the gravity-defying boy and asked him to come down. And down the boy jumped, bouncing as if he had springs in his feet as he and his grandpa walked off into the Hawaiian sunset.

Since that day, I've noticed that Crystal Children have amazing motor skills. This mirrors recent trends with Intelligent Quotient (I.Q.) tests that measure two types of intelligence: verbal and nonverbal. The I.Q. rates for verbal skills are down, while nonverbal I.Q.'s are soaring high. And overall, the collective I.Q. scores are up, since both types of I.Q. scores are tallied together for a cumulative score.

Many Crystals show remarkable motor-skill functioning, even in the face of lagging verbal skills. And these sparkling motor skills are combined with a brash fearlessness, which results in these children being brave explorers! The fearlessness seems to match the confidence that Crystal Children show in other areas, such as approaching wild animals and making psychic predictions.

Since fear is a function of the lower self—the ego—their fearlessness is one more indication of the high evolution of Crystal Children. They trust, love, and enjoy themselves while exploring this planet!

Cynthia Berkeley says that her 15-month-old daughter, Leah, is very comfortable in her body and has an amazing sense of exploration. Cynthia remarks:

> "It's almost as if Leah doesn't have any fear at all! She climbs all over everything and can problem-solve how to maneuver things with the greatest of ease. People comment about how physically advanced she seems to be. Her sense of spatial relationship is wonderful, and she was climbing up and down the stairs by herself at nine months. We play at Gymboree, and she just *loves* to climb on everything! She has no sense of fear."

Harry, whom you met in the previous chapter, has always been free of fear. His mother, Karenanne, says this was a source of worry when he was small, but (more for his mother's sake than his own) he's learned to be careful. She says, "I believe that Harry knows that he's safe, and he never worries about anything. He tells me, 'I'll be fine, Mummy.' Of course worry and fear are not part of his makeup if he's a higher vibrational soul."

Not only are the Crystal Children fearless, but they seem to gain great pleasure from exploring their physical surroundings. Tara says that her 16-month-old son, Grant, is very daring. She told me that "Grant *loves* to balance! The other day I found him standing on his fire truck, balancing on the seat. Next, he balanced himself on the steering wheel! He held his arms high up in the air and was extremely proud of his accomplishments."

Natural Instincts

Perhaps these children are more natural, more instinctual. They're more in touch with their bodies. After all, that's what the angels tell me our future looks like. Ever since childhood, I've seen visions of a world that's more natural, where technology is replaced with our own God-given abilities to communicate with telepathy. It's a world with fresh air, clean water, a tropical atmosphere, and plenty of fresh fruit and vegetables.

The new Crystal Children are a sneak preview to that world. They're definitely more in touch with their bodies!

Ellen Welch recently purchased a yoga videotape for relaxation. She says, "Since you're supposed to watch the tape before you do the poses, I put it on while I did some housework." Her four-year-old daughter, Erin, plopped right down in front of the television and performed all of the poses, stopping only to ask for certain props to help her with a particular pose. The videotape has two yoga sessions totaling about 70 minutes. Erin did yoga nonstop the entire time. While doing the poses, she said, "Mama, this is *so* good for you. We should do this every night before bed."

Erin's right—we should.

· · · ✳ · · ·

CHAPTER FIVE

Natural-Born Healers

Crystal Children carry so much love in their hearts that their mere presence has a healing effect, yet they also possess astonishingly innate skills in this area. Even very young Crystal Children seem to instinctively know how to direct energy with their hands, thoughts, and even with crystals to effect profound healings. The following stories speak for themselves, offering us glimpses into a future characterized by natural and spiritual healing.

Infant Healer

Andrea's daughter's natural healing abilities were evident during infancy. One day, Andrea was bedridden with an illness when her husband brought their seven-month-old daughter into the bedroom. Andrea says that her daughter sat there on the bed next to her, stared into her eyes, and then laid both of her hands on her stomach. "This went on for almost ten minutes, and my husband was a bit freaked out over it. When she was done, she snapped back into being a 'normal baby' and wanted to play. I was floored."

Taught by Angels

When Haley was five, she began telling her parents about the angels she was seeing and hearing. She told them that she mostly worked with the Archangel of Physical Healing, Raphael. Haley said that the Knowledge Angel and the Love Angel taught her, too. She described the angels bringing a machine into her room that taught her how to heal people's bodies. She also talked about seeing shadows around people who were sick.

Now at age six, whenever Haley is around an angry person, she puts her hand out an open window and flicks negative energy from the room. Haley's mother, Carolyn, says:

> "I love it when Haley places her hands on my shoulders, gently presses down on them, and I become calmer. Once during a ceremony we were holding, Haley got up, took the Tibetan singing bowl, and moved it over the tops of our heads. Then she came back and used her hands to open the top of our crown chakra. She did this so knowingly. She'd never done anything like this before, yet it felt so right and it was done with such gentleness, love, and compassion."

A Boy Heals His Dog

Magda says that she and her two children were devastated by the news that their dog, Gator, had a potentially fatal health condition. As Magda's daughter cried over the situation, her six-year-old son, Austin, calmly went into his bedroom and retrieved the energy wand his grandmother (a spiritual healer) had given him.

Austin then waved the crystal stone at the end of the wand over the dog. Amazingly, Gator laid down, as if the two were speaking to each other, and agreed to let the healing begin.

Austin waved the energy wand over Gator for about 30 minutes, telling him that he wasn't going to die and that he was making him better. When he was finished, Austin said to his mother gleefully, "Mom, Gator's going to be fine. I used my magic wand on him, and he's better now."

Austin (whose grandmother initiated him as a Reiki energy healer) continued to do Reiki treatments, using his energy wand on Gator for the next month. Magda reports, "Gator's now perfectly healthy without any side effects, and he and our family are happy and complete!"

She Heals Herself and Her Mother

Teresa Zepeda says, "My six-year-old daughter, Crystal, is definitely a healer!" Teresa says that Crystal has instantly healed herself more than once.

When the family went camping at a beach to celebrate Crystal's fourth birthday, the little girl started complaining of an earache. Teresa told her daughter to heal herself or they'd all have to leave the beach to take her to the doctor. This news upset Crystal, so Teresa instructed her to go in the motor home and lie down, put her hand on her ear, and ask God and Jesus to heal her. Ten minutes later, Crystal came out of the motor home and was fine. No pain, no earache! Teresa says, "Crystal is a strong-willed person. She wanted to stay at the beach so much that she made it happen."

Another time Teresa's back ached, so she asked Crystal for a hands-on healing. She placed her little girl's hands on her back, but Crystal pulled them away and said, "I don't have to put my hands on you to heal you."

Teresa reports, "The relief from the pain was immediate, as if it was never there in the first place. I've had severe back pain since I herniated some discs 14 years ago. Before Crystal's healing, I was often bedridden with back pain. Since the healing, I haven't been bedridden once, and my back only bothers me a little now and then."

All types of healing have a faith component, whether it's traditional or alternative medicine, or spiritual healing. Studies show that the healer's and the patient's faith are important variables in determining the outcome of treatments. The Crystal Children have extraordinary faith in their abilities to heal, and this is undoubtedly one reason why they're so effective at it.

Three-year-old Victoria refers to herself as "Dr. Toria," and she's already established a successful track record in alleviating headaches and backaches for friends and family members. Since infancy, Victoria's been aware if someone is injured or not feeling well, and wants to kiss it away or touch it until it's all better.

Victoria's grandmother says, "Victoria believes that you can 'throw bad things away,' and during her healing treatments, she mimics reaching into your boo-boo, snatching it up, and tossing it away, into the air. She's always been so aware of other people and their problems, and she's so certain she can fix them!"

One time Victoria and her grandmother visited a nursing home. Of course, Victoria wanted to heal all of the residents. Her grandmother recalls that it was very difficult to convince her grand-

daughter that she couldn't cure a very old, infirm person of all their problems; or that a person in a wheelchair might be in God's hands. Victoria said, very solemnly, "But Grandma, I talk to God!" Her grandmother notes that Victoria's belief in herself and her ability to change the world is amazing, and "a beautiful thing to see."

Comfort from the Crystal Children

Not only do the Crystal Children heal physical bodies, they also mend people's hearts. For example, they provide:

- *Emotional healing.* After four-year-old Lois O'Neill's brother, Jack, passed away, 50 guests attended a wake at the family's home. Lois's dad, Mick, says that instead of attending to her own grief, his little daughter spent her time walking grieving adults around the garden. Lois explained to each person that Jack wasn't really gone. Mick says, "Lois lightened their hearts with her explanation of our garden, the angels, and the fairies who live there."

- *Comfort*. Four-year-old Colin intuitively knows how to comfort a person in need. One time when Colin and his parents were visiting some relatives, one of the women became ill. Colin insisted on sitting with her in her bedroom. Even though she slept most of the time, Colin quietly sat by her side. Whenever she'd awaken, Colin brought her cold drinks, or alerted the family if she needed something. He was a true source of healing energy and assistance.

- *Compassion*. Studies show that children often avoid contact with disabled children, yet this new generation seems to break that mold. They show natural compassion for people with physical challenges. For instance, three-year-old

Zoey makes friends *predominantly* with physically disabled children. One of Zoey's playmates was born unable to walk and has a slight droop on one side of her body.

Crystal, Zoey's mother, says, "This little girl has made a considerable amount of progress since beginning school with other children, and also since her play dates with Zoey. It's been a very rewarding experience to know that there are no prejudice barriers in the eyes of our Crystal Children."

- *Counseling.* Crystals have a knack for saying just the right thing to inspire, comfort, or uplift people. Naturally optimistic, they help others see the silver linings in life's clouds.

  At five years of age, Carter is already showing natural counseling abilities. Carter's mother recalls the time her friend Ingrid came for a visit. Ingrid, a gifted hypnotherapist and artist, was feeling blue. Little Carter went up to her and said, "You're a beautiful and talented therapist, Ingrid."

Carter's mother remembers: "Ingrid thought I'd coached Carter to say that. But I told her I hadn't, and that I'd never before heard Carter use the word *therapist* or talk about the concept of being talented. All I know is that Carter can psychically pick up who needs love, and then offer it."

And offering that love is the collective mission of Crystal Children. They teach us to receive love. As their adult guides, our job is to nurture them so they'll be unafraid to love, to help them know that it's safe to talk about and feel deep emotions. We need to guide them, especially during the adolescent years, to remain their naturally loving selves.

· · · ✳ · · ·

CHAPTER SIX

Magical, Spiritual Children

Even in households without any formal religious or spiritual focus, Crystal Children talk about profound, esoteric topics. Sometimes they learn about God, prayer, angels, ceremonies, and such from their parents. But very often, Crystals possess innate knowledge about spirituality. They're little philosophers, high-priests, and priestesses. Clearly, they're tuned in to the Divine. They're also bringing in this knowledge from other lives.

Erin, three years old, strolled into the living room as her parents were watching the movie *Speed*. The film was just finishing up, and there was a scene depicting an airplane and a bus colliding in a huge, dramatic explosion. Erin thought it was a news program and that people had really been hurt. So she turned to her parents with a stunned look, got down on her knees, and exclaimed, "We gotta pray to God!" Erin's mother says, "I was impressed that a three-year-old would leap so quickly from, 'Oh, no, this is awful,' to 'We need to seek Divine intervention to help these people.'"

Erin's reaction to tragedy—even though it wasn't "real"—is heartening. It's one more indicator of where we're headed. Imagine a world where everyone turns to prayer—instead of fear or worry—in response to crises.

Crystal Children are highly philosophical, often talking about spiritual topics that seem more the domain of elders. Melissa says that her seven-year-old son, Liam, constantly asks questions that she wouldn't expect someone his age to wonder about. For instance, Liam frequently asks what a "soul body" is, who God is, and other such questions. Liam sometimes answers his own questions himself. Perhaps his queries trigger a channeled response. For instance, he'll say, "We're all God."

Melissa is grateful for Liam's spiritual quests. She says, "As long as Liam continues to be the soul he is, then the world is a better place."

Moon Energy

The Crystal Children have strong connections to the energy of the earth, nature, and the moon and stars. Like ancient Druids, Babylonians, and Egyptians, they're fascinated with starry skies and full moons.

Perhaps their super-sensitivity makes them acutely aware of the powerful healing influences of the moon. Many Crystal Children can see the moon and stars at night before they become visible to adult eyes.

In fact, *moon* was the first word that a Crystal Child named Isabella ever uttered! Her mother, Jaimie, explains, "Isabella loves the moon and called it 'moon' the first time she saw it. This was before she said 'Mummy' or 'Daddy'! I'd taken her outside on a beautiful inky-blue night, and Isabella gasped and pointed at the full moon in the sky and said, 'Ooooh, moon!' She was about nine months old at the time."

Crystal Children are clearly enamored of the moon. While other kids play with toys,

Crystals are entertained by moonlit skies. Beth says that her three-year-old son, Taylor, loves to sit and gaze at the stars and moon. He'll spend hours just sitting in his bedroom in the dark, looking out his window at the night sky.

> The Crystal Children have strong connections to the energy of the earth, nature, and the moon and stars.

These kids are also affected by the moon's cycles. Petra reports that her three-year-old daughter, Julie, normally sleeps all night without any problems. But on evenings when there's a full moon, Julie is awake for one to two hours a night.

Magical Abilities

Not only do Crystal Children have spiritual leanings and innate healing abilities, but some of them are also alchemists and Divine magicians. They defy laws of gravity, and move matter with their thoughts! Many parents shared detailed stories of their children's magical feats with me. In some cases, I was only granted permission to relate the stories under condition of anonymity. The parents feared repercussions if their children's gifts were widely discovered. Yet, as the witness to these stories, it's my opinion that they're truthful. They have the emotion, detail, and authenticity that distinguish them from tall tales. I'll present some brief examples and let you be the judge.

First, *psychokinesis* is the ability to move physical objects with one's mind or strong emotions. It also occurs when someone's personal power interrupts the electrical power of appliances, watches, batteries, or even streetlights. As you'll read here, some Crystal Children are performing amazing psychokinetic feats.

For example, there's a seven-year-old boy who lives in France whom I'll call Adam, since his mother and grandfather asked me to protect his identity. Adam speaks of life on other planets and several past lives, with details about culture, ethnic background, and language. Adam's mother says, "When he was three years old, he sat me down and told me, 'You know you weren't my first mommy. I chose you and Papa to be my parents now, and you're doing a good job.'"

Adam has frequently exhibited profound psychic abilities. For example, when he was four years old, Adam told his mother, "Oh, your father didn't go to work today. It was stormy out, so he went for a walk instead." Adam's grandfather lives in America, where there's a six-hour time difference. Since it wasn't yet Monday in America, and Adam's grandfather doesn't work on weekends, Adam was seeing the future! When Adam's mother called her father the next evening, she wasn't surprised to discover that her son's vison was true.

Adam's mother says that he also has powers over material objects. She says:

"One day Adam showed me how to light and relight a candle without a match—when we were outside in the wind!

"Adam has amazing powers of concentration and can make a rubber ball levitate. I knew that he'd been trying to do this for some time, and he finally succeeded. I heard the ball bounce on the floor and went up to his room to see what he was doing. He'd done it at least two times before I entered the room. He wanted to show me, and he did; I couldn't believe my eyes! The ball levitated a couple of centimeters off the covers of his bed and fell with a big thump, like someone had just thrown it there!"

Adam's mother told me that she's wary of other people's opinions about her son's abilities, since they live in a religiously fundamentalist community in France. Additionally, she's concerned because she believes Adam becomes depleted and vulnerable after he levitates objects. Hopefully, her fears won't be transferred to Adam and cause him to abandon his Divine magic.

၆ ၆ ၆

Another woman (who also asked to remain anonymous) recounts a similar story about her four-year-old son and four-month-old daughter. She recalls that her daughter, who was only a few weeks old, caused a wooden toy to fly through the air and land several yards from its original position. This occurred in full view of four adults and two children. The mother believes that her daughter caused the psychokinesis because she was upset that she wasn't being nursed right away. She also notes that her son was a very alert baby, able to manipulate matter around him. She recalls, "I distinctly remember that on more than one occasion as a babe-in-arms, he 'turned the TV off' when he wanted our undivided attention and we weren't giving it to him quickly enough."

ဢ ဢ ဢ

Similar to the story above, Tina's eight-week-old daughter can also manipulate electronic equipment. Tina explains: "I take my daughter to work with me, and if I have her too close to my computer, it freezes. My office partner lost her monitor the other day, and we also had problems with our printer. I'll be placing crystal clusters on all my electronic equipment to disperse the strong currency waves that my daughter emits."

ဢ ဢ ဢ

A Soul Visitation

The loving souls of the Crystal Children can also magically visit us in our dreams or meditations, like guiding angels delivering Divine messages. Laura Ainsworth was with her four-year-old granddaughter, Beth, meditating on the bedroom floor. At first, Beth sat by Laura's side. Then, as Laura continued to meditate, she heard Beth quietly leave the room. Laura says:

> "I don't know how long I'd been into the meditation when I heard Beth calling to me in a soft voice: 'Nana.' And again a bit louder: 'Nana!' I opened my eyes and gazed upon her wrapped in a blanket outside the bedroom door, and smiled. She said with a penetrating gaze and heartwarming sincerity, 'I'm here for you if you need me.'

"I went back into the meditation, and not one minute later, I heard very deep breathing, almost snoring. Beth was sound asleep across the hall in another bedroom."

§ § §

If your children aren't acting like little wizards or sorceresses, it doesn't disqualify them from the Crystal Children category. Not all of these kids perform feats of magic. However, isn't it great to know that some of them display talents that, most likely, all humans are capable of? Once again, the Crystal Children point the way to humanity's possibilities . . . and model the high road for all of us.

· · · ✳ · · ·

CHAPTER SEVEN

Connecting to Nature, Animals, and Rocks

As much as the Crystal Children seem to be from other planets and realms, they sure do bond deeply with Earth, nature, and animals. These children would rather be outdoors playing among trees, rocks, flowers, and water than anywhere else! Some parents actually have difficulty keeping their kids indoors. Other parents say that an outdoor excursion is an instant mood elevator if their Crystal Children act grumpy. Like little Saint Francises, these kids display a purity that makes animals trust them. You can practically imagine the flowers, birds, and sun singing with joy—so happy to be in the company of a delightful Crystal Child.

Four-Legged Friends

Just as music tames wild beasts, Crystal Children have a hypnotic effect upon animals. As mentioned earlier, they can roughhouse with big dogs and sharp-clawed cats and never get hurt. Animals sense the innocence of these kids' hearts. Animals and Crystal Children communicate with one another on the wavelength of love, and understand each other perfectly.

Leah, at 15 months, has already forged deep friendships with her family pets. In fact, her mother, Cynthia, says that Leah's best friend is their dog, Yogi. Cynthia says, "The first time Leah stood by herself was when she'd pulled up on Yogi to stand. Then Yogi walked away, and she stood on her own. It's amazing, because most animals let her touch them and pull on them or pet them roughly. It's like magic. Animals adore her!"

In a similar fashion, three-year-old Abbie attracts animals. Her mother, Andrea, reports: "I often find her sitting with our dog or cats, just holding her hands on them and not speaking. I'll watch as this goes on for minutes at a time. She seems to calm the animals."

Isabella, age 18 months, has twice swum with wild dolphins in Kona, Hawaii. Phillipa, her mother, says that during both swims, dolphins were very attracted to Isabella. "The dolphins came straight to her, dove down under her, and kept coming back time and again."

Wild and domestic animals alike are attracted to Crystal Children, sensing the love and trustworthiness of these special youngsters. When 18-month-old Hannah Caldwell went to the zoo with her mother, Pam, the animals stared at the little girl, instead of vice versa!

A mother gorilla at the zoo had a baby about Hannah's age. Pam says, "The gorilla and I were both breast-feeding mothers, and I felt a tremendous bond with her." The mother gorilla noticed Hannah and walked right up to the glass that separated the zoo pen from them. The gorilla and Hannah locked eyes and stared lovingly at each other. Pam recalls, "Then the gorilla looked at me and gently put her hand on the glass right by my face. I put my hand against hers. It was an incredible connection—she was so drawn to Hannah."

Eventually, Hannah and Pam bid their new friend farewell and walked to the zoo's lion area. Mother and daughter stared through the glass wall at the lions, who were sprawled out over a very large area. Pam remembers:

> "Suddenly a lioness looked up at something that caught her attention. She got up and walked over to the area, totally drawn to whatever was on the other side of the concrete wall from me. She came all the way over and was so intent and focused. I looked to see what she was so interested in, and it was my daughter! They were face-to-face, separated by the zoo's glass wall, but totally connected. She was so drawn to Hannah! It was like Hannah was the zoo attraction, not the other way around. The spectacle drew a huge crowd, and everyone wondered what was so special about this little girl that she'd capture the complete attention of this beautiful lioness."

Empathy for Nature

In addition to befriending animals, a key characteristic of Crystal Children is their profoundly deep empathy, which is particularly directed toward nature. Crystal Children feel the emotions and sensations of animals, bugs, and plants. They give voice to nature, and remind us that everyone and everything has feelings.

- Andrea says that her three-year-old daughter, Abbie, won't let anyone kill bugs—not even big, scary spiders. "God made them," Abbie tells adults who are about to exterminate insects. We often think of bugs being the domain of little boys, but female Crystal Children don't discriminate among their nature friends. They like bugs as much as they like other living creatures.

- When six-year-old Robert's parents had a pool installed in their backyard, two willow trees had to be removed for the project. At the sight of the chainsaw, Robert ran to the trees, hugging each one

in turn, and cried
huge tears for them.

- Chad, age seven, has
  shown empathy
  toward nature since
  he was a toddler.
  Once, when a leaf
  fell from a tree, Chad
  said to his mother,
  "Oh, that poor leaf
  that's falling to the ground—it left its
  family!"

> Crystal
> Children teach
> us about the
> magic of nature,
> and make us
> aware that
> everything
> is alive.

- When lizards get into his family's house,
  seven-year-old Liam gently catches them
  and takes them outside. As he does so,
  Liam tells the lizards things like, "You
  must go home; your babies are waiting for
  you," or "You need to go outside and get
  some food; I know you're hungry." Liam's
  mother says that the boy knows what
  lizards are thinking and feeling. He tells
  them not to be afraid, and they listen.

- Someone once picked a flower and handed it to two-year-old Crystal, and she became very upset. Crystal went to the stem still in the ground and tried to reattach the cut flower.

- Alice, age five, has a great love of plants and can become upset when her mother prunes plants or removes dead or dying leaves or flowers.

- Six-year-old Isaac showed his Grandma Laura a smooth pebble that he held in his hand. Isaac explained that he'd picked up the pebble from the road because he didn't want it to be run over by a car.

- Zoey, three, hugs trees and kisses leaves that have been torn or dried up.

The Great Outdoors

With their wide-open hearts and sunny dispositions, it's no wonder that Crystal Children prefer to spend time outdoors with animals, plants, and fresh air. Crystals are partial to natural beauty over artificiality.

For example, they like to take their clothes off, dig in the dirt, and inspect ant colonies. Crystal Children find beauty in nature's details, and sit transfixed for long periods just staring at plants blowing in the wind.

Conchita says that her 20-month-old son, Nathan, is a true nature lover. "We have to lock all our doors to keep him in. He prefers to have his clothes off in nature when he can. He loves playing in water and mixing it with dirt and eating it."

Perhaps one reason why Crystal Children love nature so much is that they communicate with plants and animals. Magda says that her four-year-old daughter, Taylor, constantly talks to flowers. "Taylor tells the flowers how beautiful they are," explains Magda. "She also talks with little bugs and tries to comfort them."

Crystal Children teach us about the magic of nature, and make us aware that *everything* is alive. Shawn and Keli Carpenter say that their three-year-old son, Corbin, has very significant relationships with trees. "Corbin tells us what the trees are saying, feeling, and doing," the Carpenters explain. "He's also aware of the spirit in all life and can communicate with birds, fish, plants, insects, and rocks, although it seems strongest with the trees."

And when four-year-old Colin was taking a walk outdoors with his mother one day, he stopped, looked at a tree, and leaned against it. Colin sighed and said, "Mom, I feel the tree's love; I feel its heart!"

Nature is a great mood elevator for everyone, including Crystal Children. Amanda says that if her 14-month-old daughter becomes whiny, all she has to do is take her outside. "Immediately she becomes happy and peaceful just by walking on the grass or picking up dirt."

No elaborate toys are necessary to entertain these special kids. Just take them outdoors and they're transfixed by watching rustling leaves, spiders, and birds. Rihana, 12 months, becomes cranky when she spends too much time indoors. Rihana's mother says that the little girl is endlessly fascinated by touching the trees, feeling the grass, and chasing blowing leaves.

Even older Crystal Children prefer nature to man-made toys. Six-year-old Haley wanted to de-clutter her bedroom and get rid of her unused toys, so she sold the toys at a family garage sale. Haley and her sister netted $192 from the sale. Instead of purchasing more toys, they bought a red maple tree for the family's backyard.

With this much love for the outdoors, it's no surprise that Crystals develop environmental concerns at young ages. Many of these youngsters are protective of Mother Earth. For example, five-year-old Nicky constantly reminds his mother not to waste water. He's also conscientious about electricity's effect on the environment. Nicky turns off lights when he leaves a room and won't turn them on until the sun goes down.

Crystals and Rocks

It's fitting that Crystal Children are fascinated by crystals and rocks. They're so sensitive to life-force energy. These children *know* that the mineral kingdom is just as alive as God's other kingdoms. To a Crystal Child, a beautiful rock formation is as deserving of affection and attention as a person or animal. They're all God's living creatures in the eyes of a Crystal Child.

When three-year-old Victoria visited the ocean tidepools of Southern California with her father and grandmother, she was in her element! She put her ear to the ocean rocks and talked and listened to each one. Her grand-mother says, "She drew a crowd, since it was so clear to everyone that Victoria was having conversations with those rocks."

Crystal stones have long been used in spiritual ceremonies and healing work to direct and amplify Divine energy. Quartz crystals are also used in electronics, such as radios and watches, to increase electrical signals. Some people believe that ancient civilizations used crystals for transportation and lighting, and there are theories that the Ark of the Covenant consisted of crystals infused with focused intentions of perpetual energy.

Crystal Children feel the impulses emitted by crystals, and are respectful of the crystals' magical properties and powers. Many of these children intuitively know how to work with crystals in healing work, with no formal training.

Carri Lineberry is the mother of two daughters, Shailyn, age four; and Maia, age three. Carri says that both girls love to handle their collection of polished crystal stones. Several times, the girls have displayed an uncanny awareness of the power of these crystals.

For example, Maia keeps an amethyst

geode crystal under her bed. Carri says, "I found it there one day and put it away. Maia promptly discovered it was gone, put it back, and informed me that it was to stay there."

Another time, Shailyn climbed into bed with Carri. Shailyn saw a rose quartz crystal on her mother's nightstand and picked it up. Carri recalls, "I had just purchased that crystal, and Shailyn had no knowledge of it."

Shailyn placed the point of the crystal on the center of Carri's forehead and said, "Mommy, I can fix people with this. You can do surgery with this, you know.'" Shailyn continued placing the crystal on different parts of Carri's body with the same degree of confidence you'd see in a seasoned energy healer.

Carri finally asked Shailyn where she'd learned how to use a crystal for healing, and she replied matter-of-factly, "From Jesus."

Carri remembers that the energy in the room was incredibly calm and serene. She says, "I had goose bumps. I'll never forget that morning, and the glimpse I had of another time and place."

Judy Springer's four-year-old son, Isaac, also has an inexplicable knowingness about crystals. One time, for instance, Isaac told his mother out of the blue: "You know, crystals wear out if they're kept in the house too long. If they do that, then you have to put them outside for a long, long time."

Some Crystal Children receive information about the use of crystals from their guides and angels. But other Crystals recall knowledge from past lifetimes.

Stephen and Karen Williams say, "Our five-year-old daughter, Sabrina, immediately developed a love for crystals when we first introduced them to her. She quickly learned the different types of crystals. Now she helps us select crystals to purchase."

One evening, Sabrina said she needed a crystal healing. After she'd selected some crystals, her mother began teaching her about the chakra system in the human body. Karen was about to tell Sabrina how to place crystals on her chakras when Sabrina said, "Mummy, I know where they go, I've done this all before," and proceeded to place the crystals on her body for self-healing. Karen said that watching her little girl work with crystals that evening convinced her that Sabrina's connection with crystals extended beyond this lifetime.

Perhaps the Crystal Children's connection to ancient lives is one reason why they gravitate toward time-tested healing instruments such as crystals, labyrinths, and medicine wheels.

A six-year-old girl showed uncanny knowledge about these wheels one day. Carolyn says that she was outside mowing the lawn when her daughter, Haley, said she wanted her mother to see the meditation space she'd created. Inside Haley's bedroom, Carolyn saw that her daughter had tied blankets to her bedroom furniture to create a sacred space. In the middle, Haley had placed her crystals and special stones in a circle. Haley explained to her mother that she'd been sitting in the center, meditating.

Carolyn recalls:

"The room was so peaceful, and the sacred circle she'd created was beautiful. A few nights later, Haley asked me if I'd sit in the circle of stones with her, and she told me all about healing. She shared the importance of the circle with me, had me hold a quartz crystal in my hand, and then instructed me to hold it next to my heart. Then she got up and invoked angels around the circle and asked Archangel Raphael to come into the center with us. She placed a small heart-shaped rose quartz next to where she saw Raphael so that the loving, healing energy was front and center. Haley knew what she was doing—it was incredible!"

Even if your child isn't performing healing ceremonies with crystals, you may notice that he or she has an affinity for these magical stones. Mary Marshall told me that her four-year-old son loves crystals so much that he carries them around and even sleeps with them. Mary says, "He's in preschool, and for a class project, he had to bring something to school that started with the letter *C*. He decided to take some crystals."

Petra says that when her three-year-old daughter, Julie, began having sleep difficulties, crystals saved the day. Petra recalls that Julie suddenly didn't want to sleep alone and was waking up five or six times a night. Finally, Petra had a conversation with Julie and learned that her daughter was seeing ghosts in her room.

Petra solved the problem by performing a nightly bedtime ritual with Julie. Petra now lovingly commands the ghosts to leave the room, and then she places a rose quartz and amethyst crystal in Julie's bed, as well as a clear quartz crystal on the window. This keeps the energy of the room clear of untoward visitors, and now Julie sleeps through the night.

Another mother also found that crystals helped her son sleep better. Laura Halls, a professional psychic healer, received an intuitive message to build a crystal energy grid in her son's bedroom. She placed a hermatite crystal in the exact center of the bedroom, and four rhodochrosite crystals in each corner of the bedroom. Laura then visualized an energy grid with lines of energy running between each crystal, forming a high point in the center above the hematite. She then asked that an etheric mirror be built across the top of the pyramid to reflect negativity upward, away from the room. Afterward, Laura invoked her child's angels and guides to protect him.

Laura says that her children now go to

sleep faster and sleep through the night. She recalls, "The temperature went up in my son's bedroom for two days after we made the crystal energy grid because it created so much positive energy in the room!"

Some Crystal Guidelines

Since Crystal Children have a symbiotic relationship with crystals, you may want to introduce your kids to these amazing stones. You can purchase crystals at metaphysical bookstores, crystal specialty shops, and gem shows. And keep in mind that natural crystals have stronger energy currents than the man-made varieties.

Connie Barrett, who has owned a crystal shop for many years, recommends allowing children to select their own crystals. She says that many times, kids know exactly which stone will help them feel calmer and more peaceful. Connie says:

> "One time a mother and son vis-
> ited my store. The mother began telling
> me about the child's various problems,

and the boy kept trying to tell her that he'd found the crystal he wanted.

"The mother finally turned to him, and said, 'Will you be quiet for a minute? I'm asking the lady what crystal would be best for your asthma.'

"I asked to see what crystal the boy had chosen. He showed me a rhodochrosite, a stone, which, because it's believed to help relax the muscles of the solar plexus, is recommended for asthma. I told the mother that her son had done a fine job of choosing the crystal he needed."

Children have intuitive abilities when selecting their own crystals. This doesn't mean that you can't give them crystals that you think they'd like. They'll probably like just about any crystals you give them.

If your child is still very young, remember that small stones can be swallowed. Don't leave babies alone with crystal stones, and place them out of reach. Or, purchase a large crystal with smooth edges so that a baby can't fit the crystal into his or her mouth or get cut by sharp edges. Also, explain to young children not to throw stones!

Connie says that, as important as it is for children to have freedom to choose stones that feel right, there are particular crystals that can be helpful for certain childhood conditions and issues.

- *Nightmares/insomnia:* Amethyst—place it on the child's nightstand or beneath the pillow.

- *Heartbreak or grief:* Rose quartz—hold it over the child's heart, or let it be worn as a pendant that hangs over the chest.

- *Self-esteem and self-confidence issues:* Citrine—can be worn as a ring or necklace, or placed anywhere in the room.

- *Concentration, focus, and studying:* Carnelian (for being grounded in the present) or sodalite (for clearing up mental confusion)—place in the child's study area.

- *Emotional overwhelm:* Moonstone—to be worn as a necklace pendant, or rub the moonstone over the forehead and temples.

- **Patience:** *Rhodonite*—the child should rub the stone in her hand when feeling impatient.

- **Communication:** *Turquoise* (if your child has difficulty in asking others for help); *blue lace agate* (helpful for peaceful communication); *amazonite* (helps to promote the courage to speak the truth)—especially effective when worn as a necklace or on a necklace pendant.

After purchasing a crystal, clear the former owner's energy by placing the stone out in the sunlight for at least four hours. In the absence of sunlight, you can submerge the stone in water mixed with sea salt. Don't soak the stone long in the water, as salt can erode crystal. Then, ask your Crystal Child to hold the crystal next to the heart and think of wishes or intentions to infuse into the stone. For example, he or she might intend that the crystal help with physical healings, or a better night's sleep. If any negative energy surrounds the crystal, clear the crystal again with sunlight or sea salt-water. This can be done on a regular basis.

Divine Nature

Poet Dorothy Frances Gurney wrote: "One is nearer God's Heart in a garden than anywhere else on earth." Crystal Children instinctively know this and are in tune with the Divinity of nature. Nature is their church, their temple, their place of touching, smelling, and being aware of God.

When four-year-old Colin and his mother went for a walk in a beautiful Japanese garden, the boy stopped and exclaimed, "Mom, this is so wonderful! I feel God and the angels here!"

Kate Mitchell, who owns a crystal shop in Los Angeles, reports that a five-year-old boy named Alex recently visited her store with his mother. Alex saw a large quartz crystal cluster priced at $500, and he exclaimed to his mother, "This is what I want Santa to bring me for Christmas!" His mother hesitated and said, "Wouldn't you like a Nintendo set like the other kids?" Alex answered with a determined "No!" Then she asked him, "Alex, why do you want *this* crystal so bad?" He replied, "Because it's natural, and God made it."

Rest assured that Santa brought sweet little Alex his crystal cluster for Christmas.

· · · ✳ · · ·

CHAPTER EIGHT

Angels and Invisible Friends

You might see baby Crystals staring off into space, eyes and heads focused and moving as they gaze at angels. Often these stares are accompanied by unintelligible "conversations" with the unseen world. Many parents with whom I spoke are convinced that their Crystal Children babies (who are sometimes referred to as "Crystalines") are seeing angels and deceased loved ones. Well, of course! Why wouldn't one of the most psychic generations of all time be born clairvoyant?

Many generations of humans have produced psychic babies and children. The Crystal

Children generation, however, is poised to retain their spiritual gifts into adulthood. One reason is that, in this new age of spiritual openness, parents are more supportive of Crystal Children's psychic abilities. Previous generations, frightened by all-things-psychic, condemned people who saw or heard angels.

Tara Jordan and her family customarily say grace as they sit down for supper. Shortly after her son turned 13 months old, he started calling out for Jesus during the dinner prayer.

Tara says:

> "Grant will look up as we say grace, and you can tell that he sees Jesus or angels or spirits on a different level. He'll look up and wave to what seems to be nothing. He calls out Jesus' name and says 'Hi' as if greeting him. He'll then look over at the picture we have of Jesus at The Last Supper and wave again. There's no doubt in my mind that Grant sees and feels the spirit world."

Thanks to their supportive parents and grandparents, Crystal Children retain their psychic abilities as they age. Crystal Children naturally feel an affinity for angels, since they can sense the unconditional love of the celestial beings. They also love it when their parents teach them about the angels, and they use this knowledge to tap in to heaven in an even deeper way.

Carolyn took my book *Healing with the Angels* with her during an emergency trip to the hospital when her five-year-old daughter, Haley, broke her arm. As Carolyn read a prayer for healing, she asked Haley to call upon Archangel Raphael (the Angel of Physical Healings) to be with her and help her heal quickly and take away pain. Thereafter, whenever Haley's arm began to hurt, the little girl called upon Raphael.

By the time the doctors examined Haley, they expressed astonishment at the little girl's calmness. Carolyn and her husband, Mike, were also amazed by how relaxed Haley was, and also by how peaceful they themselves felt. After all, Carolyn normally becomes tearful and very frightened when one of her children gets hurt. The angels were obviously influencing everyone in a positive way.

As the doctors put a cast on Haley's arm, Carolyn noticed a tremendous feeling of peace in the emergency room. Afterward, Haley said, "Look, Mom, my cast is green, and green is the color of Raphael for healing!"

Ever since, Haley has been talking to her angels, working with, and learning from them. Carolyn kick-started the process, and then Haley and her angels took it from there. One night, Haley began sharing the wisdom she'd learned. She sat on her knees, almost in a prayer pose, and began telling her mother the wonderful insights and great knowledge she'd gleaned from the angels. Carolyn says, "I felt like Haley was an angel, channeling this wisdom."

Carolyn related the information that Haley shared about Archangels Raphael, Gabriel, and Michael:

"First, Haley said that these were *big* angels, and their feet went all the way down into the ground, and they were like giant trees rising up to heaven. Haley admitted that the first time she saw the angels there were many in her room, and she feared they were ghosts. But then she saw their wings and knew they were angels, so it was safe.

"She said that the Angel of Knowledge was working with her. One night, she asked this angel what the word *activity* meant. The angel told her it meant 'many things happening.' Haley said the angels teach her reading and math. Her kindergarten teacher corroborated this by telling me how impressed she was with Haley's vocabulary.

"On another occasion, Haley asked me what the word *anesthesia* meant. I asked Haley where she'd heard the word, and my daughter replied that Raphael had used it while teaching her about healing the previous evening. Haley says that sometimes when she's playing in her room, she's not alone. She's playing with Raphael and the other angels."

Psychic Children, Psychic Parents

Angels are all around each of us, and the

Crystal Children are confidently communicating with them. If you know a Crystal Child, then you've got access to your own psychic-development teacher!

"As soon as Zoey was born, I started seeing angels and deceased relatives," says Crystal, Zoey's mother. "My psychic abilities really opened up." One of the reasons why Crystal Children are catalysts for others' psychic abilities has to do with their powerful love energy. This love opens our chakras, especially the heart area. We become unafraid of love, which leads us to be more aware of the loving angels' presence.

Crystal says that she began seeing orbs of light around Zoey. The orbs even show up in photographs of the little girl!

Many of the parents and grandparents with whom I spoke discussed seeing sparkling lights, aura glows, and even angels around their Crystal Children. Cindy Goldenberg says that she noticed bluish-white orbs of light around her sleeping daughter. Cindy says, "If I moved Kirsten's blanket, the orbs would fly under the blanket, still shining."

Cindy has encouraged Kirsten's clairvoyance, and says that her daughter, at age five, is very accurate in "reading" people based upon their aura colors. Cindy and Kirsten sprinkle "angel and fairy dust" over newspaper headlines so that the situations and people involved will heal. They're a good example of a parent and child pooling their spiritual gifts.

Invisible Friends

It's perfectly normal and even healthy for children to have "invisible friends"—that is, beings who are usually their guardian angels or spirit guides. When parents are supportive or encouraging of children's relationships with invisible friends, then children feel validated for having natural and God-given abilities.

Sometimes the invisible friends are archangels who help the children with important life purposes. Or, the invisible friends can be guardian angels, helping children let go of their fear. The invisible friends can even be departed relatives, friends, or even pets.

Several years ago, a woman named Melissa became pregnant by a man she adored and loved. However, the man wasn't interested in a relationship or a baby. Melissa didn't tell her young son, Liam, that she was pregnant. However, one day Liam drew a picture and handed it to his mother, explaining that it was a portrait of his little brother (Melissa only had one child at the time).

Ultimately, Melissa made the difficult choice to terminate the pregnancy, without telling Liam. About a week later, Liam said that his little brother told him, "I decided not to come yet, but I'm okay, and I love you." The little brother said that he was taking care of Melissa like a guardian angel until he was ready to be born as a child. When that time came, both the little brother and Liam would take care of their mother.

Melissa says that Liam is profoundly clairvoyant. One time Melissa did a meditation to discover who her "power animal" was (some traditions believe that we all have an animal spirit guide who's not necessarily a deceased pet). During the meditation, Melissa discovered a lioness around her. She was sitting in her big leather chair, enjoying this meditation, when Liam walked into the room. He asked how the big scratches on the chair's arms came to be. When Melissa said she didn't know, Liam answered his own question.

"Mom, you know it was your lion that put them there!" he said.

"My lion?" Melissa asked.

"Yes, the lion that follows you around, Mom. Don't you see her?"

Liam explained that he always saw the lioness with his mother, and that the big cat slept at the end of his mom's bed at night.

Melissa says, "I was amazed!" She then adds, "Thank God. I'm so blessed and honored to have my son. He's my light and my strength."

One reason why parents needn't worry about their children's psychic abilities is that these gifts can help kids heal from emotional and physical pain. They're God's self-healing abilities established in each of us.

For instance, five-year-old Sabrina was grief-stricken when a friend of hers died. She received some comfort from the angels with whom Sabrina has had a lifelong relationship.

Yet, she was immediately relieved of emotional pain when she clairvoyantly saw her friend in the spirit world.

Sabrina said that, during her sleep, she'd talked with her friend, who was smiling and standing under a rainbow. Sometime later, Sabrina's mother relayed this message to the friend's parents, who shared that her daughter's last painting was of herself standing beneath a rainbow.

Past-Life Memories

Some of the Crystal Children speak of vivid memories of other lifetimes. This in itself isn't too unusual, as kids often talk about past lives. The new and exciting development is that adults now give more permission and validity to their children's discussion of prior lifetimes. This allows the kids to keep these memories alive without wallowing in them.

When we realize that life is eternal, we lose our preoccupation with death. We also release the anxiety perpetuated by some religions about hell and damnation. And when we release those fears, we're truly free to live fully.

Here are some examples of children who

remember other lifetimes:

- Six-year-old Robert frequently talks about his "old parents," the ones he had before he came into Mommy's belly. He's described his life with them in detail. Robert told his mother that he watched from heaven as she shook the thing in her hand and it turned blue (a pregnancy test kit), and then he came into her belly.

- Beverly Moore says that her five-year-old son, Ethan, seems to remember many of his past lives. Beverly says, "Ethan talks about past lives a lot. He always says, 'Do you remember when I was your age, and you were mine?' He's told me that he was my mother once and my father once."

- Five-year-old Evan was discussing the topic of girls with Nathan, his older brother. Suddenly Nathan said, "Evan, how would you know anything about girls? You're only five years old!" Evan immediately retorted, "Oh, for goodness' sake, Nathan. I've been a woman at least 60 times!"

Some of the Crystal Children are on this planet for their first lifetime, and Earthly living can seem foreign or unsettling to them. Cathy says that her three-year-old son, William, would sit on her lap and ask if they could go home. Cathy replied to William, "But *we are* home," to which he'd say, "We are?" Finally, Cathy realized that William was referring to an unearthly preexistence, so she gently told her son, "We're here on Earth because we need to be, and home won't be that far away." That seemed to satisfy William.

ฦ ฦ ฦ

Part of our jobs as adult guardians of Crystal Children is to show them the ropes of Earthly life. That includes helping them stay open psychically, teaching them to clear away lower energies, and empowering them with knowledge. Like beautiful flower buds, we're the adult gardeners who must nurture Crystal Children into fully open bouquets.

· · · ✳ · · ·

CHAPTER NINE

A Gift for Music, Art, and Entertainment

The Crystal Children are multitalented. Not only are they loving, psychic, and sweet, but they're also naturally gifted in the arts. Many of these children have musical talents and artistic capabilities. A few show protege-like talents without having had any formal training. Once again, the Crystal Children are role models, showing us the very best of human nature.

Songs in their Heart

Many Crystals begin to sing before they speak words. In fact, Saharah's grandmother says she came out of the womb humming. Now, at six months old, Saharah doesn't say any words, but she hums in perfect tune.

Evie, another mother of a Crystal Child, says that her daughter learned how to speak through music. Evie recalls, "When Meishan, who's now two years old, started speaking, she'd just sing little songs to communicate with us. She absolutely loves music!"

Many of the parents surveyed for this book told me that their Crystal Children were innately musically gifted. For example, Cindy says that her five-year-old daughter, Kirsten, has a beautiful singing voice. This is surprising, since, according to Cindy, nobody in the family can carry a tune. However, Kirsten can instantly mimic any song she hears, with perfect pitch.

Several parents told me that their children sing constantly. For instance, three-year-old Emily continually makes up tunes, sings traditional songs and nursery rhymes, and re-creates the melodies she hears on the radio. She dances all the time, moving to any music (or sometimes no music at all!). Her mother, Wendy, plans to enroll her in a dance class when she gets a little older.

Musical aptitude is often where we see evidence of the Crystal Children's high intelligence. For example, three-year-old William knows the words to every song played on the Radio Disney station. And 15-month-old Erin taught herself how to harmonize with songs on the radio as she sings along in perfect unison.

> *Musical aptitude is often where we see evidence of the Crystal Children's high intelligence.*

Creative Artists

The Crystal Children also love to draw, paint, and create. They can entertain themselves for hours with a mere drawing pad and crayons. The high creativity of Crystal Children reflects their right-brain dominant style, which also includes being:

- aware of their emotions,
- intuitive,
- advanced in motor skills,
- philosophical,

- spiritually minded, and
- musical.

Right-brain dominant individuals think in pictures and feelings, as opposed to words. Their visual orientation gives them an artistic flair and a photographic memory. Some of their artwork comes from copying the images they see in their mind's eye.

Rosa McElroy says that her five-year-old daughter, Audrey, shows a real gift for artwork. "No one taught Audrey how to draw," says Rosa. "She's always been able to draw beautiful pictures that only a real artist would think to create. She seems above her age level when she draws, in the way she blends colors just right. Her artwork is breathtaking!"

As you can see, Audrey's mother is highly supportive of her artwork. With Rosa's encouragement, Audrey will likely blossom into a confident and highly skilled artist.

One delightful aspect of Crystal Children is how they're entertained by ordinary items. While previous generations seemed dependent upon elaborate and expensive toys to keep them happy, Crystals are content with a flower, a puppy, a pen and paper, or a moonlit sky. It's the same thing with their artwork. No expensive craft kits are necessary. Truly, this is a generation of kids who appreciate simplicity and basics. How refreshing!

For example, seven-year-old Jacob Daurham treks into the desert near his home and finds "treasures" to make crafts with. He brings home old horseshoes, railroad ties, and anything else he can use. Then he makes his own patterns for craft projects and builds them himself.

Budding Thespians

The Crystal Children may not talk a lot—especially when they're young. However, they're definitely expressive people! They express strong emotions and opinions through their eyes, body movements, songs, and artwork. They also express themselves through dramatics. Not the temper-tantrum drama-queen or -king-type of dramatics. No, the Crystal Children use drama as a playful form of expression, in the way that humans must have enjoyed Shakespearean productions before radio and television. These children take us back to our roots.

Many of the parents and grandparents surveyed for this book said that their Crystal Children showed no shyness in front of audiences. Most were like three-year-old Victoria, whose grandmother said:

> "Victoria has infinite poise and self-confidence. She's taken gymnastics and dance classes since she was one year old. She loves to perform, especially dance. She's never experienced shyness or stage fright, whether the audience is made up of hundreds or thousands or a few dozen people. It has always been a joy to watch her dance or do gymnastics, as she loses herself in it and is so happy that she glows. She practices endlessly, lost in the joy of the music and the movement."

Crystal Children are fun to be around, and one reason is that they're highly entertaining people. One woman said that she's enthralled by her three-year-old daughter's ability to do impersonations. She told me that her daughter can pick up the most dramatic voice inflections, mannerisms, and phrases someone uses, and then incorporates these elements in order to imitate the person. "She's so good that we can immediately recognize who she's imitating. She doesn't do it in a mean or even humorous way; it's done purely as an observation, or for her own entertainment."

And it's not just little girls who enjoy dressing up and performing. Male Crystal Children are getting into the act as well. Catherine Poulton says that her five-year-old son, Kylan, is always getting into character, and changes his clothes about ten times a day!

"I'm constantly picking up his clothes off the floor because he pulls everything out of his drawers to look for costumes for whatever character he's being," says Catherine. "He also cuts up his pillowcases, clothes, sheets—whatever he can find to create new costumes. He just loves to act."

Catherine says that Kylan also draws every day, often sketching pictures of the characters that he plays. "He makes up his own superheroes with their own magical powers. These characters are often based on himself."

It sounds like Kylan remembers his magical capabilities and may be practicing for the time when Crystals are the superheroes of our world. After all, they've got what it takes!

· · · ❋ · · ·

CHAPTER TEN

Angel Babies

"Delightful," "A real angel," "A gift from God." This is how parents and grandparents describe their Crystal Children. And while everyone has Divine qualities, these kids seem to express their higher selves more than previous generations. Here are some characteristics that Crystals bring to the world:

Affection: This is another reason why delayed speaking isn't enough to warrant an "autism" label. These kids are super-affectionate, almost to the point of being clingy. Autistic people are physically distant, definitely not cuddly.

Mary Marshall notes that her five-year-old son seems to be happiest when the two of them are together, just hugging and laughing. He loves to snuggle with his mom. Mary says, "He was very clingy when he was little and still reverts back to that behavior at times. For instance, if we're in an unfamiliar or uncomfortable place, he wants me to pick him up and hold him, and then he buries his head in my shoulder."

Crystal Children don't limit their affection to family members. Stephanie and Mark Watkeys say that their 13-month-old son, Bryn, wants to kiss most people he meets. "He's very loving and affectionate to everyone," they explain.

Happiness and joy: These kids emit positive energy via their facial expressions, postures, words, and actions. They're a joy to be around because they uplift those around them.

Lauren Stocks says that her six-year-old son, Carter, has a completely positive demeanor. She says, "It's as if Carter is just here to love." On almost a daily basis, Carter says, "Oh, Mom, it's a beautiful day!" and he'll cheer her up when she's down.

Everyone comments on Carter's cheerful attitude, which is common in Crystal Children. For instance, Beth and Michael's son, Taylor, has had three different baby-sitters. All of them have said the same thing about the three-year-old boy: "He's such a bright spirit!" Everyone says that Taylor warms their hearts.

His parents say, "Overall, Taylor's a delightful child who brings us nothing but joy and love. When we sense his spirit, we have hope that the human race will find peace, and that violence will be eliminated on this planet."

I received more stories on this joyful aspect of Crystal Children than any other. And lest you think that these are parents who are gushing because it's their offspring, many of these moms and dads have other children whom they find challenging. Here are some of the comments I received from parents talking about their Crystal Child:

> "A lot of people say that being with Celeste makes them feel more peaceful. Often, she spontaneously goes to people who suffer in some way and sits by them or plays with them."

From Nadia Leu, regarding her 18-month-old daughter, Celeste.

"She's the sweetest, most loving spirit I've ever encountered. She goes right up to strangers, takes their hands, and you can just feel the love she's sending! A very sensitive, passionate, attentive person." From Wendy Weidman, regarding her three-year-old daughter, Emily.

"My Robert is a six-year-old 'angelheart.' He has love for all people. He wants to comfort every person he sees in need. If a friend's hurt, Robert's totally caring. He wants to give something to every homeless person on the street. Robert's a sweet, loving soul, and it seems as though the sun radiates from within him." From Michelle, regarding her six-year-old son, Robert.

Love and respect for elders: As if sensing the wisdom and peacefulness that comes with age,

Crystal Children are magnetically drawn to older people. They adore their grandparents, and also bond with elderly strangers.

Mary and her three-year-old daughter, Haley, frequent an ice-cream parlor that has an outdoor eating area. During their last three visits there, various elderly people have been seated outside eating by themselves. In each case, Haley walked right up to the elders and sat beside them. She didn't speak until she was spoken to, but Mary says that Haley was practically cuddling each of the seniors. She obviously sensed their need for love and companionship, and volunteered to meet that need.

In the same vein, Conchita Bryner says that her two youngest children (a son, 20 months; and a daughter, 5 years) are attracted to senior citizens as if there's a special kinship.

Conchita's family recently held a memorial for the ten-year anniversary of their children's paternal grandmother's death. She recalls:

> "Since my youngest daughter didn't know her grandma, she asked me lots of questions about her before the memorial. She knew we were taking

flowers to the grave, so she made her own bouquet. To my surprise, she also asked her older sibling to write down a poem that she'd created on her own. As she read the poem at the memorial, my husband and I were in tears—she told her grandma she missed her and that she was in her soul."

Forgiveness and peace-keeping: What the world needs now is forgiveness and compassion, and the Crystal Children are shining examples of turning the other cheek. Where their older Indigo Children brothers and sisters have a warrior spirit that keeps them fighting for causes, the Crystal Children have adopted a Gandhi-like style of dealing with conflict. For example:

Gloria Powell-Frederickson, the mother of two Crystal Children and one older Indigo Child, says that during conflicts, she sees glaring differences between the generations. She says, "During arguments, my Crystal Children will give in and walk away, completely unbothered and full of forgiveness. But my Indigo Child prefers to stick to the argument and fight it out."

Corbin, age three, has learned about conflict resolution through his connection to nature. He always talks about the trees and the things they say or do. Whenever he hears people speaking in a negative tone of voice, Corbin says, "Please talk like the trees." By that, he means to speak with gentleness and love.

Mei, age two, never hits any of her playmates, although they hit her. She simply retorts, "No, don't hit me—I'm your friend!"

Denise Christie says that her five-year-old daughter, Alice, can become very hurt if someone is cruel or spiteful to her: "Alice has no comprehension of why someone would want to do such a thing. She's so pure that I don't even think she realizes when she's being bullied."

ʃ ʃ ʃ

The Crystal Children emanate love in all their actions and deeds. They're indicators that the human race is evolving above petty differences and squabbles. They've living examples of operating from the higher self and not the ego.

Yet, Crystal Children aren't entirely problem-free offspring for their parents. I asked parents to tell me about any challenges they'd encountered with these kids. For the most part, the issues reported were minimal. Even so, a few showed up repeatedly, as you'll read about in the next chapter.

· · · ✳ · · ·

CHAPTER ELEVEN

Eat, Sleep, and Be Picky

Any human characteristic can be viewed in a negative or positive light. For instance, stubbornness can also be called tenacity or "stick-to-it-iveness." And assertiveness can also be called "pushiness." I think you see my point.

A similar observation can be made about Crystal Children and the choices they make. On the one hand, anyone who's operating from higher chakras holds high standards for themselves. When people open their heart chakras and truly love, they tend to attract (and be attracted to) situations and persons with loving energy. An open-hearted person is repelled by situations or relationships involving violence, negativity, impurities, loudness, or anything jarring.

The Law of Attraction holds that we draw people and situations to us that mirror our dominant thoughts and beliefs. For example, if we believe that people are basically good-natured, we'll attract sweet and loving friends.

As we travel the spiritual path, we may change our circle of friends, the way we eat, and other lifestyle choices. Our new choices mirror our evolving self. And Crystal Children, who are born far along the spiritual path, are naturally attracted to—and attract—situations of the highest spiritual energy frequencies.

This results in the Crystal Child appearing to be fussy or picky. However, another way to look at it is that the child is "discerning." A discerning person has high self-esteem and cares enough to choose friends, meals, movies, jobs, homes, and such that feed and nurture the body and soul.

Diet and the Crystal Children

Once I fully immersed myself in spiritual studies, my appetite for food and beverages shifted almost immediately. I received strong inner guidance to eat more organic fruits and vegetables, and fewer animal products. I've been a complete vegan (meaning I don't eat any meat, fowl, fish, or dairy products) since 1997, and I'm extremely happy with this lifestyle choice.

Many of my students, audience members, and readers report having received similar inner guidance. Although they may not leap to veganism, people on the spiritual path generally eat fewer processed foods; and avoid red meat, white sugar, and refined flour.

The angels say that humans are evolving toward becoming less dependent on eating for energy and nourishment. According to the angels, we'll first become vegetarians, then we'll become "raw foodists," eating only uncooked fruits and vegetables. Next, we'll switch to juices, which are easier to digest. Finally, we'll become "breatharians," and receive all of our nutrition from the prana life-force in the air. All of this will enable us to become more intuitive, and also help us adapt to Earth's changing food supplies as we get away from processed foods and move toward harvesting fresh produce.

Well, the Crystal Children are already there. They've already evolved their taste buds to very high levels. Uncooked organic fruits and vegetables have the highest life-force energy of any foods. So, it's no surprise that Crystals prefer vegetarian diets. Yet, it's all in how you view this situation.

Some parents see it as a problem. For instance, one mother told me that she struggles to get her four-year-old son to eat "real meals." She's going against the natural grain of these children, which is to "graze" on smaller, more frequent meals of healthful foods and juices. Nutritionists say that grazing is a healthful way of keeping blood-sugar levels balanced and to avoid binge eating.

Many eating patterns reported by parents of Crystal Children show that they're very much in tune with their bodies. So if parents can trust that their kids' natural appetite preferences balance out with their nutritional needs, then power struggles at mealtimes won't occur. These children's predilections for food can be trusted, judging by the stories I've received.

For example, many of the Crystal Children are self-made vegetarians. Seven-year-old Jacob, for instance, refuses to eat meat—even though his mother isn't vegetarian and tries to get him to eat it.

The main reason why Crystals won't eat beef, fish, or fowl has to do with their empathy for animals. One two-year-old boy said, "Eating fish is bad because they die when they're taken out of the water." And Shailyn, age four; and Maia, age three, are self-proclaimed vegetarians because they say it's not nice to kill animals to eat them. Two-year-old Mei says, "Yuck, dead chicken," or "Yuck, dead cow," whenever she sees fowl or meat.

Parents who worry about their children's nutritional needs will be happy to know that the American Dietetic Association has deemed vegetarianism to be a healthful and balanced way to eat. Vegetables, grains, soy products, nuts, and legumes contain sufficient protein for a healthy youngster's body. Most dietitians, nutritionists, and medical doctors also recognize that vegetarianism is healthful. After all, animal products are associated with heart conditions, high cholesterol, obesity, osteoporosis, and other health concerns.

Three-year-old Corbin's parents constantly receive compliments on how calm and relaxed their son is. They partially attribute

Corbin's relaxed temperament to his diet of organic foods with no refined sugar.

Many parents report that their children would rather drink their meals than eat them. For example, Kelly, mother of five (three of them young Crystal Children), says, "My children are vegan and eat little sugar. They have a very liquid diet. They show a natural aversion to meat and heavy foods and constantly want water." And three-year-old William prefers drinking juice to eating solid food. Parents who worry about their children's diet can always make smoothies in a blender, with soy or rice-based protein powder containing vitamins and minerals (available at most stores in the health-food section, or over the Internet).

Along the same lines, quite a few mothers report that their Crystal Children want to breast-feed beyond their first year. And most parents report that eliminating sugar from the diet helped their children's moods and energy levels to stabilize. One mother said that if her five-year-old daughter eats anything containing chocolate, she becomes wild and practically uncontrollable.

Sleep Patterns

In my survey, I asked parents to describe any challenges they've had with their Crystal Children. By far, the single most frequent answer given involved sleep patterns. These children have high energy and don't want to miss a thing while they're sleeping! They may also be reflecting a higher state of evolution when humankind needs fewer hours of sleep. Regardless of the reason, there's definitely something going on in this area.

Crystal Children are so sensitive that anything stimulating can lead to insomnia. Thirteen-month-old Bryn's sleep pattern is the only challenge his mom has faced with her son. She says, "Since birth, he's been very alert. Bryn takes in everything around him with great intention. This leads to him getting overstimulated, and then he finds it hard to settle down to sleep."

To nap or not to nap seems to be a very individual decision. Erin's parents found that if she took naps, she was up all night. Since they eliminated her naps, Erin now sleeps through the night and seems happier in the mornings. Her mother says, "We now use the afternoons as structured playtimes for making treats, craft projects, or watching a favorite video."

Other parents said that naptime was essential. If Victoria, age three, skips a nap, it takes days for her to recover so that she's feeling well and in sync.

This is an area where caretakers will want to personalize a sleep program according to the child's individual rhythms and needs. For other sleep concerns, parents have come up with some unique solutions:

- Colin, age four, is very psychically connected to his mother. She says, "As a baby, and until about a year ago, he'd wake up crying immediately after I'd wake up from a bad dream. So I started a nightly routine of visualizing the cord between us as a chain, and I'd separate it at two of the links (it didn't feel right to me to sever a cord between us)." This ended the nighttime wake-ups.

- Another mother, who'd tried everything to get her daughter to bed, also tried cord cutting, and says there was an immediate improvement. She says, "If I notice the old bedtime antics returning, I clear my chakras, and things return to normal! It was an amazing discovery for us!" [Note: To cut the cords of fear that can cause problems, just hold the intention and ask the angels to snip them for you. That's all it takes. However, if you want details on cord cutting, please consult my book *Chakra Clearing*, published by Hay House].

- Robin Rowney is the mother of twin Crystal Children sons who didn't sleep through the night as infants. One night, exhausted from a sleepless night with her twins, Robin prayed desperately for help. She soon noticed a sound coming from her son Zack's crib. She thought he was waking again for another feeding, so she quietly listened to see if he'd start calling for her. She looked over at the crib and noticed a light growing brighter and brighter hovering around his bed. At the same instant, Robin realized that Zack was actually giggling. She sat forward to make sure what she was seeing was real, and the giggling grew so loud she thought he'd wake his brother.

Robin says, "The light looked to me like a golden-yellow haze. There was no defined shape, but I knew with my heart and soul that this was one of Zack's angels. A feeling of calmness and peace came over us." Robin and her boys slept soundly after that.

- For a while, four-year-old Shailyn refused to go to bed, so her mother began giving her Reiki energy treatments while tucking her into bed, saying, "Now, I'm tucking you in with beautiful, golden light, and the angels are here to protect you and stay with you." Shailyn now goes to bed without any struggles.

- Crystal's mother discovered that if her daughter had sugar close to bedtime, she wouldn't go to sleep. So sugar at this time of night has been eliminated—as have the sleeping problems.

- Haley was plagued with nightmares about witches and dark images, so her mother taught the little girl how to clear her energy space. Now Haley says to any untoward spirits: "If you're not of God, you must go!" Haley also visualizes a bubble of white light around her home, along with a golden dome of protection. This has alleviated the nightmares and has empowered young Haley.

- Kathy DiMeglio used a combination program to help her daughter, Jasmyn, to sleep. Kathy says that Jasmyn's sleep problems stemmed from a combination of fear of being harmed during the night and separation anxiety from her parents. So Kathy began playing the *Chakra Clearing* audiotape at night (many parents find it soothing, and it clears the energy of rooms quickly). She also began praying with her daughter, and talking to her about the archangels at bedtime. Then Kathy took Jasmyn to the store and let her select a stuffed animal to sleep with. Afterward, Kathy cut her cords of fear to her daughter. Jasmyn now sleeps beautifully, and her parents don't worry about this area anymore.

Potty Training

There wasn't a clear pattern regarding toilet training Crystal Children. Some parents said it was a breeze, and that kids practically taught themselves what to do. However, other parents are still struggling.

Abbie's mother says that her daughter takes her time with most things. She says, "Abbie spoke late for the most part, walked after her first birthday, and *refused* to be potty trained until she was more than three years old."

Another woman told me that her son's toilet training was challenging because he wants to do everything for himself. She said, "He's extremely stubborn, making potty training a challenge. He's quite aware of the ability to do it; he just chooses his own ways and when."

Parents said that giving clear explanations to their Crystal Children helped them to understand *why* toilet use is important. Some Crystal Children refuse to comply until they understand why.

Picky or Super Organized?

Are the Crystal Children intuitively trained Feng Shui artists who know that disorganization creates energetic discord? Or are they just prone to neurotic perfectionism? Again, I would opt for the answer signaling spiritual progress. However, when you actually live with a Crystal Child who insists that everything be *just so*, you might agree with the latter explanation during moments of frustration.

I received dozens of stories about Crystal Children's organizational skills, and how particular they are about their rooms, their belongings, and their clothing. For instance, seven-year-old Hannah is very sensitive about the comfort of her clothing. Her socks and shoes must be positioned perfectly, and her clothes must be soft or she won't wear them. True nature children, many Crystals prefer nudity to clothing.

Crystal Children like neat and organized bedrooms, and some of them don't mind doing the work themselves. Three-year-old Victoria keeps her room very clean, which is no small accomplishment given the piles of toys, clothes, books, and stuffed animals she owns.

Crystals also enjoy organizing their toys during playtime. For instance, three-year-old Taylor loves to line up his blocks and toys into shapes of crosses, airplanes, or alphabet letters. One time he placed all of his toys into a continuous line throughout the house. When it was done, he exclaimed, "It's beautiful!"

Two-year-old Mei loves to place things into categories, like grouping together her baby dolls and Mommy dolls. She loves to put her dinosaur models into a long line, from the smallest to the biggest.

Sometimes the Crystal Child's organizational leanings border on perfectionism. For example, three-year-old William won't use a crayon if it's broken, and he won't eat food that's "messy" with sauce. And seven-year-old Jacob insists that building blocks be placed into precise positions.

Again, it's all in how you look at the situation. You could call it perfectionism—which has a negative tone. I like the way Wendy Eidman calls it "high creativity" when she describes her three-year-old daughter, Emily. Wendy says:

"Emily's attention span is unlike anything I've ever witnessed before. She'll get into a groove coloring or playing, and she won't be disturbed until she's done. This works to my advantage when we're picking up pine cones in the backyard. We have this giant pine tree that drops hundreds of cones every fall. When we pick them up, Emily stays on task better than anyone else in the family. My son gets bored after five minutes, but an hour later, Emily's still out there picking up cones!

"It bothers her to leave a job unfinished. After we'd cleaned the yard one day, she was playing on the swing set, and every once in a while she'd spy a stray pine cone that had escaped our attention earlier. She'd get off the swing, or stop playing basketball or whatever else she was doing, then she'd walk over to the pine cone, pick it up, and deposit it in the cart! Emily is all about consistency. She likes to know what to expect; she likes to have things the same way all the time.

"Emily gets upset, for example, if her brother decides he wants to sit in her seat at dinnertime, that sort of thing. Every night at the table, we have the same conversation. We go back and forth across the table, asking each other, 'So, how was your day?' Usually my husband, Kirk, answers, 'My day was very work-y.' But the other night, Kirk answered, 'My day was very busy!' And Emily got upset. She said, 'No, Daddy. Your day was very work-y!'"

Crystal Children love consistency. In a world where everything seems in flux, who can blame kids for wanting stability and predictability? Sounds refreshingly healthy to me!

Taking Their Time

In the new world, we won't run our lives by clocks and calendars. We'll use inner timing to direct our actions. Through synchronicity, not appointments, we'll arrive at exactly the right place at the right time.

Well, the Crystal Children are already ruled

by inner clocks instead of outward time mechanisms. This can be frustrating to parents who need to keep a schedule. One thing's for sure: Parents of Crystal Children must develop a lot of patience—which is one of the lessons these children help us adults to learn.

Jennifer says that her seven-year-old son, Jacob, takes his time and doesn't rush for anyone or anything. Jennifer says that it's not that Jacob is mentally slow, it's just that he does things deliberately because he wants them a certain way. He operates from his own schedule, not others'.

Three-year-old Abbie is the same way. Her mother says, "She does things in 'Abbie Time,' and not necessarily when her preschool teacher wants her to. She hates schedules and prefers to be a free spirit. I'm not sure how that will work with her school time."

Crystal, the mother of three-year-old Zoey,

> *Crystal Children are already ruled by inner clocks instead of outward time mechanisms.*

says, "I find that you need a lot of patience with the Crystal Children, because they're old souls who take their time looking at everything, inspecting it, and then giving you feedback on what they think. Zoey sits until she figures out how to tie her shoes, do her buttons, brush her hair, and such. I try to maintain a high patience level because I understand her need to take her time. She's never in a hurry and doesn't like to be rushed."

The Crystal Children know that it's healthier to stay centered and calm rather than getting lathered up over the fear of being late. They already know that time isn't real, and that it can be bent and warped so that you'll always arrive on time—even when appearances suggest otherwise.

Deep Bonding and the Need for Attention

Crystal Children have a special bond with one or more of their parents or grandparents—whoever can understand them on a deep level. Once that bond is formed, the Crystal Child doesn't like to be apart from that person. Crystals are dependent on that adult for comfort, understanding, and cuddling. These kids may develop separation anxiety because they're afraid that other people won't understand. These kids may also fear that other children or adults may be mean-spirited, and the sensitive Crystal Children try to avoid pain by sticking with a trustworthy adult.

Timothy says that his six-month-old daughter, Julia, always wants to be held. "We can't lay her down for a minute," he says.

Pam says that her daughter, Hannah, age four, "came in with huge abandonment issues. She doesn't want to be alone at all, especially when it comes to being away from me."

Some parents see the metaphysical basis of this seeming clinginess. Carri Lineberry says that her three-year-old daughter, Maia, is extremely attached to her. Carri says, "I sense that my relationship to her is very important. I think of myself as her 'grounding force' or something like that."

· · · ✳ · · · ·

CHAPTER TWELVE

Advice from Parents, Teachers, and the Crystal Children Themselves

As a parent, grandparent, or teacher of a Crystal Child, you have a sacred and vital mission. You spiritually contracted to guide this soul through the delicate balancing act of retaining a high spiritual frequency with amazing gifts of telepathy and sensitivity . . . while at the same time assimilating into Earthly life. Your job isn't easy, but fortunately you have lots of help from Earthly and celestial angels.

Those whom I surveyed for this book were happy to pass along their tried-and-true advice based on their own personal experiences

Angels and prayer: Cynthia Berkeley says she's found it very effective to mentally ask her children's guardian angels to help soothe and calm her kids when they become overly irritated, especially when driving.

Understand that they're visual: Right-brain dominant people have visual memories instead of language-based ones. For instance, they'll memorize how spelling words *look*, instead of how they sound phonetically. Catherine Poulton says it helps her to remember that her five-year-old son, Kylan, processes information differently. When he was two years old, Kylan struggled to remember his alphabet, but then one day he was flipping through a magazine and stopped and pointed to a picture. "That's George Washington," he said correctly. This is when Catherine realized the extent of Kylan's visual processing.

Explain, don't force: Forcing a Crystal Child only leads to a power struggle. Pam Caldwell says that her four-year-old daughter, Hannah, is very sweet and easy to get along with . . . unless you try to force her to do something against her will. "But once you explain the logic behind it, Hannah will usually comply, or come up with a better solution," says Pam, who's found that it works best to talk to Hannah as if she's an adult, using age-appropriate language.

Penny, mother of a Crystal Child, agrees. "Allow them to be different, and don't force them into the 'normal' mold. Don't force them to talk, since it's possible to communicate with your children more instinctively. They'll talk when they're ready, when they see a need to talk verbally. Usually that will occur when they're interacting with other people who don't seem to understand their unique way of communicating."

Attachment Parenting: Several of the parents whom I surveyed credited "Attachment Parenting" as a style of upbringing that was particularly helpful for their Crystal Children. Attachment Parenting is a philosophy that advises parents to physically and emotionally bond with their child through being sensitive and responsive when the child cries, breast-feeding, carrying the infant in a baby sling, sleeping with the child, and providing a gentle home environment. Many books and Internet sites discuss this parenting style.

Bring animals into the acting-out situation: Here's a clever idea from Misty: "Whenever my two-year-old daughter, Leah, acts out, I tell her, 'The cats are watching you!' This calms her down immediately." Leah doesn't want to lose the felines' respect!

Live and let live: Melissa, mother of seven-year-old Liam, says, "I'm not strict. I'm not a slave driver. I allow my son to be who he is. Liam instinctively knows what chores need to be done, and he does them. There's no arguing or yelling. I'm honest and forthright with him, and he returns the favor. We're a happy, casual, and loving family, and we're functional in our dysfunctions."

Another mother named Sue, concurs: "These children need freedom to run and be. When they come home from school angry, it's because they're fed up with being caged all day; they need the freedom to feel their feelings."

Take care of yourself: Kathy says, "Parents of Crystal Children need to engage in their own routine of yoga and or meditation, and have moments of quiet reflection to become aware of their own Divine guidance. Keep a journal. Write letters to your Crystal Children—they'll not only be an amazing gift for when they're older, but it would also assist you with keeping a record of the miraculous incidents that occur over the years."

Talk _to_, not down: Crystal says that her three-year-old daughter, Zoey, acts out if she senses that someone's patronizing her or talking down to her. It's important to have discussions with Crystal Children using the same degree of respect that would be accorded to a dear friend.

Toning and chanting: Sue, the mother of two Crystal Children, says that she and her husband, Darren, do nightly chanting as their children go to sleep. The children now request it, saying, "Mummy, can you please do that _oohhh_ stuff on me?"

Schooling: Parents who can provide home-schooling, or send their children to Waldorf or Steiner schools, report great success with their

Crystal Children's level of happiness and learning potential.

A mother of a four-year-old Crystal Child says that her son attends a Waldorf kindergarten, and that she's noticed positive changes in his self-esteem, sense of social order, and imagination. (For information on Waldorf and Steiner schools, please see **awsna.org** in North America; **steinerwaldorf.org.uk** in the U.K., **steiner-australia.org** in Australia, and consult the Internet directories for other countries.)

If schedules or budgets don't allow for these options, Michelle is a great example of taking another approach. She says that her six-year-old son, Robert, is way ahead of a lot of his classmates. "He's very bright and inquisitive, so we do extensive homeschooling in addition to his schoolwork." Michelle says that Robert loves anything creative and thrives on having structure and schedules. Several parents said that when they helped their child with studying, the results were immediate.

Meditation: Catherine, mother of five-year-old Kylan, says, "My son loves to meditate and pray."

Eastern exercises: Tai chi, qi gong, yoga, and karate are wonderful outlets for youthful energy, and good tools for teaching Crystal Children to work with their own and others' energy.

Catherine's son, Kylan, loves his karate classes. "It teaches him to use his inner power effectively," she explains. "He has a great teacher, and they're not doing it competitively. Plus, karate teaches Kylan how to build a protective force field around his body so he can be empathetic without taking on other people's stuff (he's highly sensitive). It teaches him great grounding and clearing exercises, too."

Pay attention and tell the truth: Denise, mother of Alice, age five, says, "Always pay attention. These kids don't like to be ignored. Never bend the truth or lie to them; they know a lie every time and can get upset if they catch you in one. Never break a promise; keeping your word is very important to them."

Patience: Andrea, mother of three-year-old Abbie, advises parents to have patience with their Crystal Children. She says, "They're not like other kids, and probably have much more to offer if given the chance—that is, not medicated to 'fit in' with what society thinks kids should be like."

Consistency: Many parents say that their Crystals do better with a consistent eating and sleeping schedule. Studies show that children feel safe when they know what to expect. Mary, mother of a five- and six-year old, says, "Getting my children to bed at the same time each night, along with lots of affection, makes a positive difference."

Learn from them: Cynthia, mother of two Crystal Children, reminds us that Crystals are our teachers. She says, "We can teach these kids how to function in this third-dimensional reality and how to play the game, but really, they're here to teach us so much more beyond that. If you're not coming from the heart, the kids know. If you expect the kids to be naughty, guess what? They will be. Watch your own integrity and expectations. They can read you like a book and play with that."

Visualization: Since Crystal Children are highly visual, you can help them manage their moods and manifest their intentions by using visualization exercises. Here's a wonderful one that Rosie Ismail, a primary school teacher in England, uses in her classroom. She says:

"During the past four years, I've worked with healing and colors, using visualizations in my personal life. When I realized how effective visualizing the color pink is, I began introducing this into my classroom and watched the wonderful and effective results it yielded for young children. Pink is a healing, loving color that creates peace and harmony for oneself and projects this to others.

"This simple technique of visualizing I call 'The Magical Pink Light.' I ask the children to close their eyes and take five or six deep breaths along with me, slowly releasing the breath on the exhale. Next, I ask them to visualize pink magical light at the bottom of their feet, going 'round and 'round their body. I tell them it doesn't matter if they don't see the magical pink light, but that it's powerful and to just think about it. I tell them to imagine this pink light as very magical and see it going around them like a warm blanket. I ask them to make a wish in this very magical pink light and to breathe it in, and then we end by taking two very deep breaths. I then guide the children to open their eyes, stretch their arms, and say, 'That felt good!' I find that children are much calmer, happier, and more loving after the visualization."

Energetic assistance: These sensitive, psychic children need our help! They're like sponges, absorbing other people's energies (including those of well-meaning parents). David Morelli is a professional psychic who teaches children's spirituality classes at the Psychic Horizons Center in Boulder, Colorado. He also works as a Montessori schoolteacher. David says:

"One of the methods I teach children in my class is to imagine making a bubble in between their two hands, putting the 'yucky' energy in the bubble and clapping their hands to

pop it. They can put the energy of anything—their parents, teachers, or friends—in a bubble and pop it. After they make their bubbles and pop them, I then ask them to imagine happy golden energy above their heads filling in their whole bodies. This puts new energy back in to replace the other energies."

Just love them: Gloria, the mother of two Crystal Children and one Indigo Child, puts parenting into perspective when she says:

"I've learned that love is the most important thing of all. It's important to be patient and nurturing. Keep in mind that we aren't really here on this earth to master mathematics. Smiling and laughing with your children is just about the best feeling there is, so do it! When milk spills on the floor, make funny faces. When it rains outside, dance in it with your children. Love, love, love them!"

From the Mouths of Babes

Several Crystal Children also offered words of wisdom for adults:

Audrey, age five: "I would like this book to get people to understand us."

Crystal, age six, was asked by her mother what she'd like to tell people. She said, "Love. Love and help people, and be kind."

Robert, six: "All I can say is that I wish everyone in the universe (if there is life on other planets), good life, good heart, and good food. For all you grown-ups to help Crystal Children, you must protect them, play with them, and read with them."

When his mother asked Colin, age four, what he'd like to tell people, he said, "That God and the angels are with them always, even when they're scared."

Haley, age three: "I ask my angels to bring me dreams full of light before bed when I say my prayers."

Hannah, age seven: "The pot of gold at the end of the rainbow disappears, so be thankful for what you have."

Jacob, age seven: "For the future, everyone needs to know that they'll come back after they die."

Kylan, age five: "I would like to say about the planet, that it has love in it and joy and a heart. People can help themselves by putting up signs on their walls like to be happy and tape it on the wall. The sign should say: BE HAPPY!"

· · · ✳ · · ·

ABOUT THE AUTHOR

Doreen Virtue, Ph.D., is a clairvoyant metaphysician who holds Ph.D., M.A., and B.A. degrees in counseling psychology. The former director of a teenage drug and alcohol recovery program as well as other psychological programs, Doreen now works with Angel Therapy in her writing and teaching activities.

The bestselling author of *The Care and Feeding of Indigo Children*, Doreen's other titles include *Messages from Your Angels* (book and oracle cards) and *Healing with the Angels* (book and Oracle cards).

She lectures worldwide and has appeared on numerous television and radio programs, including *The Oprah Winfrey Show*, CNN, *The View*, *Beyond with James Van Praagh*, *Body & Soul Australia*, and *Good Morning America*.

For information about Doreen's workshops and products, please visit: **www.AngelTherapy.com**.

இ இ இ

OTHER HAY HOUSE TITLES OF RELATED INTEREST

An Indigo Celebration: More Messages, Stories, and Insights from the Indigo Children,
by Lee Carroll and Jan Tober

The Indigo Children: The New Kids Have Arrived,
by Lee Carroll and Jan Tober

The Journey Home Children's Edition,
by Theresa Corley—based on the parable inspired
by KRYON and written by Lee Carroll

Practical Parenting,
by Montel Williams and Jeffrey Gardère, Ph.D.

Seven Secrets to Raising a Happy and Healthy Child:
The Ayurvedic Approach to Parenting,
by Joyce Golden Seyburn

〜 〜 〜

All of the above are available at your local bookstore,
or may be ordered through Hay House directly:
Tel: 020 8962 1230
Fax: 020 8962 1239
www.hayhouse.co.uk

JOIN THE HAY HOUSE FAMILY

As the leading self-help, mind, body and spirit publisher in the UK, we'd like to welcome you to our family so that you can enjoy all the benefits our website has to offer.

 EXTRACTS from a selection of your favourite author titles

 COMPETITIONS, PRIZES & SPECIAL OFFERS Win extracts, money off, downloads and so much more

 LISTEN to a range of radio interviews and our latest audio publications

 CELEBRATE YOUR BIRTHDAY An inspiring gift will be sent your way

 LATEST NEWS Keep up with the latest news from and about our authors

 ATTEND OUR AUTHOR EVENTS Be the first to hear about our author events

 iPHONE APPS Download your favourite app for your iPhone

 HAY HOUSE INFORMATION Ask us anything, all enquiries answered

join us online at **www.hayhouse.co.uk**

 292B Kensal Road, London W10 5BE
T: 020 8962 1230 E: info@hayhouse.co.uk